Justice in Life and Society

Justice in Life and Society

How We Decide What Is Fair

Virginia Murphy-Berman, PhD

MP MOMENTUM PRESS
HEALTH

Justice in Life and Society: How We Decide What Is Fair
Copyright © Momentum Press®, LLC, 2017.

First published in 2017 by
Momentum Press®, LLC
222 East 46th Street, New York, NY 10017
www.momentumpress.net

ISBN-13: 978-1-60650-779-7 (print)
ISBN-13: 978-1-60650-780-3 (e-book)

Momentum Press Psychology Collection

Cover and interior design by S4Carlisle Publishing Services Private Ltd., Chennai, India

First edition: 2017

10 9 8 7 6 5 4 3 2 1

Printed in the United States of America

Dedication

This book is dedicated to the wonderful students I had the opportunity to teach in the seminars I offered on the topic of social justice at Skidmore College. My students had lively intellects and great curiosity. They loved to question and challenge each other to go deeper and deeper into analyses of whatever subjects we were probing. Many of the questions included in this book, in fact, were taken from points that my students raised during some of our class discussions. I thank them for their great creativity and the passion with which they approached this topic.

Abstract

If somebody asked you whether life was fair, how would you respond? In this book you will learn how to critically think about this question of justice in our lives. You will learn that people mean many different things when they talk of a just or fair outcome. For instance, have you gotten what you deserve? Have you been listened to and treated with respect? Have your rights been protected? Have you been fairly or unfairly privileged? Were you sufficiently rewarded for your contributions? Did you receive just or unjust punishment if you broke the law? Were you given a raw deal by the government?

These are tremendously important topics to consider in the contentious times in which we live. Turn on any TV or follow any debate on social media, and soon you will find that people are arguing about what is just in a particular situation. In this book you will be given new ways of thinking about these justice debates. In addition to getting quickly up to speed on the research and literature in the area, you will also have a chance to practice applying what you learn by analyzing topics like the right to free universal health care or the morality of the death penalty. This book could be used as a main text in a seminar on social justice or fairness in life, or each chapter could serve as a standalone module. The text could also be supplemented with other original source material for those who want to go deeper into any of the presented subjects.

In Chapter 1 the topic of distributive justice is reviewed. Distributive justice concerns how to fairly allocate resources in society. Procedural justice, or the fairness of the processes we use to make decisions, is discussed in Chapter 2. In Chapter 3 the topic of retributive justice, or the fairness of our assignment of punishment to those who violate society's rules, is taken up. And, finally, in Chapter 4 the subject of societal justice, or ideas about human rights and the necessary relationships that should exist between individuals and the governing state in a just society, is discussed. This book is a must read for anyone who wants to be able to thoughtfully reflect on the important and complex justice questions of our times.

Keywords

Death Penalty, Deservingness, Distributive Justice, Fairness, Justice, Human Rights, Just Punishment, Privilege, Procedural Justice, Purpose of Prison, Restorative Justice, Retributive Justice, Social Justice, Societal Justice

Contents

Foreword...*xi*

Preface ....*xiii*

Acknowledgments.. *xv*

Introduction ....*xvii*

Chapter 1   Distributive Justice..1

Chapter 2   Procedural Justice..35

Chapter 3   Retributive Justice 59

Chapter 4   Societal Justice 87

Summary...*107*

About the Author..*115*

Index *117*

Foreword

Many of our most vexing current political disputes revolve around questions such as the following: What kind of society do we want to create and support through our democratic processes? How should we understand, rank, and apply concepts such as *competition, individual merit, equality, compassion*, and *respect*, both within our own nation and throughout the world? How do we locate ourselves socially with regard to others? And, perhaps most importantly, what would it mean to construct and nurture a society that was truly just and fair to all? What would it look like? What would be its fundamental organizing principles? And how could those principles be put into effect? Would everyone in such a society necessarily have pretty much what everyone else has, or could different individuals legitimately occupy different "places" within a society that is still "fair" overall? Moreover, what should be the appropriate "cost" to an individual who violates the norms of such a society?

Since the time of Plato, Western philosophers and, more recently, political scientists have grappled with such questions. In doing so, they have argued that the concept of *justice* is a primary element in the quest to understand ourselves as social beings. In the 19th Century, the Jesuit priest Luigi Taparelli added to this conversation by coining the term "social justice," which he understood in both political and theological terms. This concept remains controversial today, as do virtually all the specific articulations of *justice* that have ever been proposed. In short, we still live with the paradox that although we use this notion on a daily basis, we nevertheless find it challenging to determine how best to articulate its many dimensions and implications.

Psychologists have joined this discussion most recently still. Through empirical research, they already have made meaningful contributions to our understanding of how different notions of *justice, fairness*, and the like actually play out in the real-life course of human affairs. In this highly accessible book, Professor Murphy-Berman provides a helpful and engaging overview of this important body of work. Her clearly stated aim is to help her readers—most especially students—not only to come to appreciate the scope and products of this psychological research, but also to see for themselves how the results of these investigations might apply to situations that anyone will find recognizable.

In short, *Justice in Life and Society: How We Decide What Is Fair* is not only intellectually engaging and provocative, but could not have been more timely. It should be required reading for both voters—young and older—and the political leaders we are charged to elect. I happily commend it to your attention.

Philip A. Glotzbach
President
Skidmore College

Preface

I have long been fascinated by ideas about justice. What do we mean by the term *justice*? How is personal justice (or fairness) different from societal justice? Why is justice so important to us? Why as children and as adults do we think the statement "You are not being fair" should carry such weight and should cast aside all doubts about whether or not we are on the right side of any argument? As a psychologist, my goal was not to look at abstract philosophical concepts about justice, but rather to probe how individuals actually think about justice in their everyday lives. In addition to doing research in this area, I also had opportunity to offer college courses on these subjects. These courses were fun and challenging to teach. I learned that when people use the words *just* or *fair* they can mean many very different things and that this can cause problems. Arguments, for instance, can reach impasses if we just talk past one another. Emotions can take precedence over reason. We can become so gridlocked in our own way of looking at things that we can fail to really hear what others are saying. One of the things that helped my students get past these kinds of impasses in debate was to learn to define their terms. What, I would ask them, do you mean when you use the word *just* or *fair*? What assumptions about justice or fairness are you making? What are the theoretical foundations you are using to support your positions? Reflecting on these questions allowed students to examine their opinions more analytically. Another thing that facilitated students' ability to think about justice-related topics in a more comprehensive manner was being able to practice arguing on all sides of any posed questions. For instance, we might be holding a debate on the fairness of providing free universal health care to all. There are good arguments on both sides of this idea. To get this discussion going, I would ask students to put forth persuasive arguments for positions with which they personally disagreed. At first they hated doing this. However, as we progressed through the course they got better and better at it.

They learned to relax and to find it interesting to try to articulate how someone else might see a particular issue from a perspective other than their own. Many students said that these types of exercises helped them sharpen their own beliefs and opinions.

This book grew out of some of the spirited debates I had with my students in these classes. In a brief book I wanted to lay out for readers some theoretical frameworks for thinking about justice and to pose some applied fairness dilemmas. Learning to think critically about these issues has never been more important. My hope is that readers will find this task both challenging and intellectually satisfying.

Acknowledgments

First, I want to thank my husband, John, for patiently supporting me during the sometimes crazy process of putting this book together. John not only offered me wonderful encouragement throughout this whole task, but also carefully read and reread each chapter I wrote and gave me incredibly helpful feedback on my work. For this I am forever grateful. I also want to thank Joan Douglas and Mark Fondacaro for the time they took to look over several drafts of this book. Their suggestions for improvement helped me make it a stronger and better book.

Introduction

Setting the Stage

This book, "Justice in Life and Society: How We Decide What Is Fair," will bring together a variety of different academic perspectives concerning key ideas and research on the topic of social justice. Social justice will be discussed mainly from a psychological perspective. This means that the major questions we will raise will concern how individuals actually perceive various aspects of justice in their everyday lives, not how justice should be considered in some ideal sense. The approach, thus, will be more descriptive than prescriptive. The idea of justice will be examined in terms of the fairness of the distribution of resources in society, the procedures for making decisions about individuals, the allocation of punishment for those who commit offenses against the law, and the safeguards put in place to preserve and protect human rights. Multiple issues will be raised, such as, what does the concept of deservingness mean? Who does and does not "have merit"? How should we understand the idea of privilege? Who should be punished and for what in society? What does it mean to be guilty of something? What are the basic human rights that all should possess? Are all human beings entitled to treatment with dignity and respect? And, finally, what actually do we mean by the term justice *itself*? Let's start with this last question.

What Is Justice?

Justice is a social construct. It is not something that exists "out there" like a tree or an orange. We cannot taste it or see it or touch it. In this sense, we create the ideas of justice or fairness, and we do this together. We decide that we will call a certain type of situation fair and another type of situation unfair. We then create rules to help us determine whether this or that particular situation qualifies one way or another. All of this means that we impose meaning on our world. We use language to develop constructs that help us interact and negotiate with each other more effectively. It is interesting, in this regard, to consider whether ideas of justice are a uniquely human invention. The answer is we are not sure. There are some studies (Brosnan 2006) that suggest that higher primates such as monkeys who live in cooperative groups may have some primitive ideas about fairness. Leaders of such groups, for instance, have been shown to forgo gathering food for themselves to make sure that others in their group are adequately fed. But does this show a concern for fairness or simple group survival? It is hard to be certain because it is difficult to define precisely what standards of evidence we would require to prove this one way or the other. This problem, by the way, is not one that occurs only in work with animals. Researchers also struggle to understand what we, as humans, mean by this rather complicated term *justice*.

When we think about this, it is important to note that justice can be defined at different levels. In this book we use the terms *fair* and *just* interchangeably, although some writers such as Goldman and Cropanzano (2014) have suggested that the concept of justice sometimes has a broader scope of focus than the concept of fairness. Particularly when the term *social injustice* is used, it often refers to some larger structural features of society that serve to systematically disadvantage groups, rather than to more limited, negative personal actions.

But what is justice at its basic sense? We do know what justice is not. To say someone treated you unfairly is different from saying that someone made you feel uncomfortable or did not give you what you wanted. It is also different from saying that you did not receive what you expected or what you would have liked to have received. Rather, at their core, justice judgments seem to be tied to perceptions of dignity and deservingness. The rage stemming from assessments of unfairness consists of a feeling of a lack of rightness and of justification. Of course, assessments of justification are always a bit murky. For instance, if I get hit by lightning or slip on the sidewalk and injure myself, is this simply an unfortunate or unlucky occurrence or a completely unjustified and unfair event? How I answer these types of questions to myself can have a powerful effect on my behavior and emotional reactions.

Most conceptions of justice are also comparative at some level. To think about this we might consider how we would see the world if we grew up alone on a desert island with no human contact. Imagine that on some days we had sufficient shelter and on other days we did not. On some days we were physically very comfortable and on other days we were quite uncomfortable. Though we might grumble against these changes in our daily condition, it is hard to imagine that we would find them to be unfair. What would this concept even mean to us in this context?

What Are Different Types of Justice?

So far we have talked about rather general definitions of justice. When we say something is not fair we can actually mean many different things by this statement (Sabbagh and Schmitt 2016). For instance, we may mean that we do not think that we received a fair outcome in some situation. These outcomes could be a range of benefits such as money, health care resources, food, shelter, grades in school, or costs such as a salary cut or taxes. This type of fairness is referred to as distributive justice and will be discussed in more detail in the first chapter of this book. As we will see, perceptions of distributive unfairness usually occur when we think that we receive too little of some desired resource or incur too many costs; but, interestingly, there are times when receiving too many benefits of some type can also be perceived as unfair.

Another type of fairness refers not to perceived fairness of outcomes, but rather to the fairness of the process whereby outcome decisions are made. This type of fairness is called procedural justice and it answers the question, "How was I treated?" This is quite different from the question of "What did I receive?" In Chapter 2, we will examine the topic of procedural justice at greater length. We will learn that our perceptions of the fairness of our treatment by others can sometimes exert just as powerful an impact on us as our assessments of the fairness of the resources we obtain. Why this is so says a lot about our psychological nature as human beings and what it takes for us to feel that we have some value and a sense of worth in life.

A third type of fairness that will be examined concerns the fairness of the allocation of punishment when transgressions occur. This is referred to as retributive justice. Here we look at who should be punished for what and why, in what kind of manner, and in what kind of situation. We will also consider the purpose of punishment and the impact that different types of punishment systems may have both on the alleged violators and victims, and on society at large. In addition, we will consider what a society might look like that had no formal punishment systems for those who disobey its laws. Is such a society possible? Would it be a good society in any sense? These are some of the issues we will take up in Chapter 3.

Finally, in Chapter 4, a fourth type of fairness that will be considered involves an analysis of human rights and entitlements. This type of fairness, that is sometimes called societal justice, goes beyond examination of fairness in specific exchanges or interactions to explore basic rights and entitlements that we should possess simply by virtue of being human. Here we will look at such things as how and if we can define human rights, and what types of procedures we may need to have in place to guarantee our expression of these rights. We will also look at such issues of whether certain types of rights are truly universal and if group rights are different from individual rights.

Each of these various topics will be considered in the context of justice dilemmas that individuals face in their day-to-day lives. The emphasis will be on applying justice theory and research to real issues that confront us as a society. Thus, in addition to a research review, hypothetical case studies and policies will be presented that allow practice in critically analyzing a variety of justice problems from a range of perspectives. These case studies and policies will deal with issues such as income inequality, access to health care services, rights to a quality education, the death penalty, victimless crimes, dealing with suspected terrorists, the special case of rape, cultural clashes in rights expression, and group versus individual rights. The purpose of including these applied exercises is to stimulate lively, balanced, and informed debate, not to promote particular positions on the issues presented. So let's get started.

References

Brosnan, Sarah F. 2006. "Non-human Species' Reactions to Inequity and Their Implications for Fairness." *Social Justice Research*. 19 (2): 153–185.

Goldman, Barry and Russell Cropanzano. 2014. "Justice and Fairness Are Not the Same." *Journal of Organizational Behavior*. 36: 313–318.

Sabbagh, Clara and Manfred Schmitt, eds. 2016. *The Handbook of Social Justice Theory and Research*, New York, NY: Springer.

CHAPTER 1

Distributive Justice

Abstract

In this chapter the topic of distributive justice is discussed. Distributive justice concerns decisions about how to fairly allocate resources in society or considerations of whether individuals have gotten the outcomes they deserve in life. Individuals' deservingness calculations have been found to be complex, and they often involve comparative assessments with others. Although sometimes people who receive a disproportionately large number of benefits experience great discomfort, individuals have also been found to be very good at employing various types of justification strategies that allow them to rationalize why they deserve to receive such benefits.

Major chapter headings include the nature of deprivation, rewarding merit while recognizing effort, paying attention to other fairness standards, dealing with privilege, considering luck, and special cases of deservingness. Each of these major sections is further divided into several subsections.

The Nature of Deprivation: I Want What You Have

We all want to receive our fair share of resources in life. But how do we determine what our fair share is? What causes us to think that we are not getting what we deserve? Why do many people feel more deprived today than people did 50 years ago, even though standards of living have risen dramatically over the years (Cassidy 2013), and the number of possessions people have has increased astronomically?

The answer to these types of questions is that a sense of justice or injustice is, as we have noted, comparative in its essence. That is, what tends to bother us is not so much what we have in any absolute sense, but what we have relative to others (Crosby 1976; Crosby 1982).

A way to think about this is to imagine a situation in which everyone had exactly the same meager level of resources. Let's say that everyone in the world had access to only one bowl of rice a day. This would mean that everyday all of us might suffer in an absolute sense and feel hungry and dissatisfied. But would we feel that this was unfair? Probably not. However, the context and meaning of this situation might change dramatically if we suddenly noticed that the people next to us had access to two full bowls of rice daily as contrasted with our one meager bowl. At this point, we might not only feel uncomfortable with our one bowl, but also feel jealous and angry at these other people for having more than us. Thus, our experience of deprivation is relative (Masters and Smith 1987; Olson, Herman and Zanna 1986; Smith, Pettigrew, Pippin and Bialosiewicz 2012). What often "gets us" is not that we have so little, but rather that we have less than others.

So what is going on here? What happens when we compare our lot with others? Why does it bother us if we think we come up short in this process? What seems to occur is that the comparison process evokes a sense of deserving in us (Walster, Walster and Berscheid 1978). That is, when we compare ourselves to another who has the thing that we want, we begin to question why that person has it and we do not. We begin to compare our attributes to that of the other person. If we believe we are at least as worthy as the other person, we may shift from saying that "we simply would like to have this particular thing" to asserting that "we deserve it." This is a big shift. Wants or desires morph into entitlements. I "would like" becomes "I should have." I "should have" becomes "it is unfair that I do not have."

But to Whom Should I Compare Myself?

Let's look some more at this process. We know, of course, that there is a tremendous variation in the distribution of resources like food, housing, and luxury goods around the world. There is variation in the things we have, in fact, even within our own small neighborhoods and workplaces. So to whom do we compare ourselves? Surely there is always someone in the world who has more than we do. If we feel upset about each one of these individuals, we would live our lives in a constant state of discontent. To stay sane, we have to be selective in choosing our comparison targets. We have to pick people whom we think are close enough to us in some ways that in a fair world we would have similar outcomes (Olson, Herman and Zanna 1986). Thus, I may not feel upset when told that Bill Gates, the founder of Microsoft, makes more money than I do, but I might react with some discomfort if told that my roommate in college just obtained a very well-paid position at Google headquarters while I am still working as a waiter to pay off my college bills. This feeling of being upset might be enhanced if I recall that we had the same major in college and I always received better grades than did my roommate and always worked a bit harder. The key idea is that I will feel badly if you have more than I do on some dimension that is important to me if I think I *deserve* what you have. In these instances, I may not only react emotionally, but also take some concrete actions to try to alter what I may see as my unjust situation. This may be particularly the case if I feel outcomes can be reasonably changed and if I feel powerful enough to put such change in place. If, on the other hand, I view myself as being too weak and powerless to affect positive change, the negative emotions evoked by perceptions of injustice may simply result in feelings of alienation and frustration or acting-out deviance (Smith and Pettigrew 2014). This sense of deprivation can also be triggered by comparing ourselves at two different points in time. That is, if I once was quite wealthy and now I am very poor, I may feel more deprived now than if I had always lived in poverty.

What is ironic in all of this is that when people begin to feel more empowered and entitled, they may also begin to become more critical of their world and more upset by their own position in it. One might say greater entitlement increases the scope of one's sense of deservingness. Thus, if I was a woman in the 1950s and I held a secretarial job, I might not have become upset if I found out that my boss made 50 times as much money as I did. My boss (who was always male) would simply not be a relevant comparison target for me. However, for my great granddaughter in 2016 such a situation might be more intolerable. This is because norms have changed over time about the role of men and women in society, and shifts have occurred in notions of to whom one should and should not be able to legitimately compare oneself.

What If Everyone in My Group Is Deprived?

There is also another way to think about the sense of deprivation. Up until now, we have been talking about a sense of personal deprivation at the individual level. A sense of deprivation can occur at a group level, as well. In this case, I may look around and notice that not only do I have less than you do but also, and perhaps more importantly, everyone in my group has less than everyone in your group. Some authors refer to this latter state as a sense of fraternal deprivation and the former as egotistical deprivation (Runciman 1966). These are very different experiences. With egotistical deprivation I may feel quite upset with my individual circumstances and, perhaps, feel motivated to take some personal action to rectify my situation. However, if I experience a sense of fraternal deprivation, I may be additionally inspired to look to my group to protest against a more generalized feeling of injustice. I become not just an individual person who is fighting to retain my own sense of dignity, but a representative of a group of people I may feel is being systematically oppressed. Our comparison becomes my group versus other groups. Our sense of deservingness expands its boundaries.

The key question, of course, is what causes this to happen. There has been considerable research on this topic (Ross 1982; Van Zomeren, Postmes and Spears 2008), and several things are striking about the findings from this body of literature. First, for a sense of fraternal deprivation to develop we need to forge a very strong identity with our group. We need to begin to think of ourselves not just as a particular person, but rather as a person who is a member of a group of people who have been deprived. We additionally have to believe that change is possible, and we have to think that our group deserves this change. So both identity and efficacy intermingle to give individuals a sense of justification. Interestingly, often when things actually start to get better for oneself and for members of our group, expectations concerning what is possible may rise and our sense that we deserve more and more may increase. This is talked about in terms of the phenomenon of "rising expectations" (Buechler 2016), and it plays an important role in fueling the process of social change.

Rewarding Merit While Recognizing Effort: The Dilemma

What Counts as Merit?

We have been talking about a sense of deservingness deriving from the process of comparing oneself with others. But how do we make these comparisons? What types of attributes in others and in ourselves serve as useful comparison standards? Early social justice researchers examined just this question. They came up with an elegant idea. What we are searching for, these researchers suggested, is an experience of equity in which the outcomes we receive are perfectly proportional to the contributions we make (Adams 1965; Walster, Walster and Berscheid 1978). For example, if I picked two barrels of apples and you picked four barrels, then a fair outcome would be for you to make twice as much money from this apple-picking effort as I do. A fair world, thus, would be balanced just like a mathematical equation in which my outcome-input ratio would be equal to your outcome-input ratio. If my input is greater, so too should be my outcomes. This formula, known as equity theory, seems intuitively quite satisfying and reasonable. Those who contribute more get more—plain and simple.

What About Effort?

There is a rub, however. Defining "contributing more" or "doing more" is not always as simple as in the apple-picking example presented above. How do we decide on the value that should be given to effort and the quality of my contributions (Milne 1986; Sadurski 1985)? Let's say you pick three barrels of apples but I pick only two. My apples, however, are carefully selected to be non bruised and of perfect shape, while your barrels are filled with apples that are small and brown in color that have to be discarded later. Who has contributed more in this case? Let's look at it this way. What if I was in the army and my task was to clear mines from a field? Imagine that I did this at great risk to myself for over 8 hours a day for a week. In this process, I cleared a few mines and saved a few of my fellow soldiers from great harm. However, one of my buddies who was quite good at mechanical things worked only 1 hour the whole week, but during that time he fixed some part of the mine-sweeping equipment to make it much safer and much more effective. Who made the greater contribution in these two cases? Who deserves more rewards or praise?

The above examples bring up the issue of how merit and effort may relate and should be weighed when we think about what is fair. To bring in a personal example, I often have had students who would tell me that they deserved a good grade on an assigned paper because they spent so many hours working on writing it. Should a grade on a paper depend on how long we spent working on it? Is that fair? As another example, I had a roommate in college who was very good at math and we took a calculus course together. She would study about 5 minutes for the various math exams we had in that course while I would study about 5 hours. She ended up getting a better grade in the course than I did? Was that fair?

But What If I Am Very Young?

As we can see, it is not always so easy to clearly determine the nature of merit. This can become even more complicated. Evaluating merit appropriately may depend on the context of the situation and may vary at different points of our lives. When we are very young, for example, effort may be rewarded because we are seen as being still in the learning stage of life. We want to be rewarded for just trying. There may come a point, however, when "just trying" hard is not enough. What, for instance, should my reward be if I am 45 years old and working on a job in which I try very hard but never master the required job skills? Is it fair to count the great effort I make when salary decisions are made?

Does Fault Make a Difference?

We can also consider the factors that may be affecting my contributions and effort. Should it make any difference, for instance, if you knew that my lack of effort was related to the fact that I recently had been very ill and did not feel well much of the time? Or perhaps my lack of ability to master the job skills was related to the fact that I stay up and drink alcohol every night or that I grew up in a very poor environment in which educational standards were quite low. Should any or all of these facts color the way the resulting contributions are judged?

Research suggests that people do react differently to different reasons for poor job performance (Knight and Stemplowski 2011). In general, negative evaluations are reduced the more the substandard performance is seen as being due to factors outside the individual's control.

Other Fairness Standards

Is Merit All That Matters?

In addition to the above, some justice researchers have speculated that merit or equity is not the only legitimate standard to use to fairly distribute resources to others (Deutsch 1975). Different distribution principles appear to support different types of values and goals (Buttram, Folger and Sheppard 1995) and fit more clearly in different types of interactions (Barrett-Howard and Tyler 1986). Use of merit as a standard of distribution promotes competition among individuals and differentiates people from each other. It also motivates people to work hard and vie with each other for rewards (Deutsch 1985). This may be a good result in something like a business transaction or an athletic contest, but merit may not be seen as being appropriate to use in all circumstances.

What About Equality?

Another distribution standard that may be considered fair in some situations is allocating on the basis of equality. For instance, if I am a mother of young twins and I am trying to decide how to allocate food between these twins at the family dinner table, I probably would not feel it was fair to use a merit standard to do this. I would not say because on a particular day one child worked harder on his or her chores than the other that he or she should receive more to eat. Rather, in this case, the fairest way to distribute the food among the two children would be to give each an equal share, regardless of each one's contribution to the general family welfare. When we distribute on an equality basis, we convey the message that all people are equally deserving and that distinctions among individuals are not important or relevant. Rather than promoting competition or personal rivalry among individuals, use of this type of fairness standard soothes relations among group members and promotes a sense of harmony (Deutsch 1985).

Getting What I Need

A third distribution standard that researchers have found individuals to consider fair in certain types of situations is allocating on the basis of need. For instance, if I had three children and one of these children was very sick and two others were quite strong and healthy, I might think it was fair to give the most nourishing food to the child who was the weakest and who needed food the most. This might be particularly the case if I had only a limited amount of this nourishing food. The neediest child would not really earn the right to the food, but he or she would benefit from it the most. Giving on the basis of need has been found to promote a sense of compassion for others. It sends a message that group members will take care of each other (Deutsch 1985).

Thus, different types of justice standards are seen as being more or less appropriate in different types of situations and are used to fulfill different types of goals. Interestingly, we often think it is fairer to use either equality or need in many types of family contexts when we do not want to promote a sense of hierarchy or difference among individuals. Use of merit seems more fitting in many economic or strictly social exchange situations when we want to maximize competition in order to increase individual effort and improve the quality of outcomes.

The Scope of Justice Concerns

A question we can raise when we think about use of these various standards is what is or should be the appropriate scope of my justice concerns. This becomes particularly important when we are using a need standard to direct our allocation decisions. Who among the needy are most deserving? Should we (or can we) give basic resources for survival to everyone who exhibits need at a certain level, even if that might mean taking away resources from ourselves or those who are closer to us in our own group or circle? What is the range of our moral universe here?

Researchers have found that individuals make complicated calculations to decide these types of questions that involve trade-offs among different values (Laham 2009; Opotow 1990; Reed and Aquino 2003). For instance, the need to be totally unbiased and equally fair to everyone in an objective sense may collide with our special sense of commitment to our own families or our communities. There is also some research that suggests that we simply do not empathize with individuals as much or perceive them as deserving when they are not from our own background and/or group (Haslam 2015; Huo 2002). In this case, we define them as "the other" and our fairness commitment to them diminishes.

Case Studies for Further Inquiry:
Different Justice Standards

Now you will be given the opportunity to analyze some hypothetical case studies involving different types of allocation dilemmas involving different distributive justice standards. Try to analyze these from a variety of different sides and perspectives. Draw on information presented in this chapter to back up your arguments.

What Is Merit?

The first case example concerns the nature of merit. Imagine the following:

> *A woman named Samantha works at a company in a small town in the United States where she holds the position of office assistant to the vice president of operations. In this role, Samantha unofficially runs the vice president's office. She schedules and presides over meetings, makes initial contact with company clients, sets the company agenda, and handles all office crises that occur. Samantha's salary is equivalent to the salary that other individuals in her small town receive for similar type of work. Another individual named Jason works at a construction firm in a bigger city in the United States. In his job Jason organizes and schedules construction assignments and allocates personnel to construction sites, as needed, to complete job requests. His salary is also roughly equivalent to what others in his geographic area make for*

similar type of work. Jason, however, makes about twice as much per hour in wages than does Samantha.

1. Does this situation seem fair to you?
2. What questions would you have to ask to determine if it was fair or not?
3. Does it matter that each of them is getting a salary equivalent to others in their city who do the same work?
4. Is it enough to just let the market place set salaries or is this sometimes unsatisfactory?
5. How could the different types of merit that each worker contributes to his or her job be fairly evaluated?
6. Would it make a difference if you are reminded that, on the average, women are paid less than men for similar work.

Evaluation of Need

This case example concerns the nature of need. Imagine the following:

Two potential liver transplant recipients are patients in the same hospital. Both have very severe liver disease and both have a limited projected life span without a liver transplant. Patient 1 is a 76-year-old former jazz musician who at one time had a drinking problem. He has had chronic liver disease for some time and has experienced much pain and agony from it. He has a wife and three children and five grandchildren. Patient 2 is an 18-year-old girl who was just recently diagnosed with a rare form of liver disease. She also has a number of other debilitating conditions that put her in very fragile health. She is not in great pain at the current time, but she is very sick. Patient 2 is unmarried and has no brothers and sisters. Her mother is a single mom who raised her daughter alone. The hospital has only one liver available at this time and the hospital staff decides that the fairest thing to do would be to give the liver to the patient who "needs" it most. They decide to give the liver to Patient 2.

1. Is the hospital's decision fair?
2. What criterion would you use to decide this?

3. What other questions would you want to ask?

4. Should outcome prognoses, degree of suffering, age or other factors be taken into consideration when one considers need?

5. Can "degree of need" ever be completely fairly determined?

A Quest for Equality

The third case examines the meaning of equality in education. Imagine the following.

> A grade school in the United States has just instituted a program of equality in its classes. According to this policy, when any athletic or academic competitions are held at school, no winners or losers are announced. Rather, all of the children receive a similar medal for participation, with their "special contributions" noted on the medal. This is done to ensure that all children feel equally rewarded for trying. After this policy was put in place, two children at this school took part in a race. One child, Joey, finished the race first and set a school record for speed. Another child, Sammy, finished last and actually walked the last couple of yards of the race to the finish line. Both received the same participation trophy.

1. Is it fair that both Joey and Sammy received the same trophy?

2. What goals might be served by giving both child equal trophies?

3. What harms (if any) might be done by this?

4. Is this an appropriate situation in which to use an equality standard of fairness? Why or why not? Would age of the children matter?

What About Privilege?

We have been talking so far about reactions to a sense of deprivation or the feeling that one has not received as many resources as one deserves. In these situations people sometimes assert that they have not been treated fairly. They did not get what they should have or to what they were entitled. As we shall see, the other side of the fairness equation, or the notion of being privileged, can be complicated, as well.

How Can We Define Privilege?

First, we can ask what exactly does it mean to be privileged. Similar to other ideas related to fairness, privilege is comparative in nature. For instance, a standard of living that would be defined as being quite privileged 50 years ago in the West might be seen as being somewhat average or below average today. A standard of living that may qualify as being privileged in one culture may not qualify in another culture. So a state of privilege means different things to different people at different times. One way to get around this dilemma of the relative nature of privilege is to limit its meaning to a particular context. I may say, for example, that I am relatively privileged if I have more resources or things than my peers do at a particular point in time. Perhaps I have more books, computers, cars, and houses than most others do. But this definition raises new questions. For instance, how much more than others do I need to have in order to grant me a privileged status? Who are my relevant comparison peers? And when does privileged become "over privileged"? Answers to these types of questions are, to some degree, in the eyes of the beholder.

What Does It Mean to Earn Privilege?

When we discussed distributive fairness in an earlier part of this chapter, we defined it in terms of an equity formulation. That is, we suggested that a sense of distributive fairness occurs when the ratio of my outcomes to inputs are seen as being matched to yours. Some types of privilege do not cleanly fit this equity model. For instance, I may say that I am privileged to have you love me with the implicit assumption that your love was not really earned by me. Or I could talk about how privileged I was to have kind and understanding parents, again with the assumption that I did not really do anything as a child to deserve this level of understanding. These types of privileges are what we might call special favors. We would not say that these types of privileges were unfair, just that they were not given to us because of something we did.

But sometimes individuals do speak of earning their privileges. They may say, for instance, that they have lots of material resources, not because they were simply given to them, but because they earned them through their hard work. Some writers see this kind of earned privilege as not only fair but also good for society. According to this view, if people believe that their efforts will be amply rewarded, they will have more incentives to work hard and to produce more. Individuals who are less advantaged can also look up to the privileged as role models who show them what can be achieved through great industry and perseverance. Outcome disparities among individuals here are not viewed as markers of an unjust system, but rather as motivators for achievement (Lamont 1994).

One question, of course, is to what degree this system of earned privileges can be fairly implemented. Even if we all agree in principle, for example, in the value of a merit-based society, putting a fair merit system in place is often difficult. And sometimes fairness considerations and other social values may collide. For instance, in the United States in addition to valuing merit models of fairness, we also value individual autonomy and freedom of choice to reward or not reward whom we want. If I am an owner of a company I may feel that I have a right to hire my daughter over more qualified strangers simply because I love my daughter and I feel that I can do what I want with my own company. I may also feel that I have a special obligation to promote the welfare of my own family. So in this case my sense of duty to my family and my valuing my freedom of decision-making may eclipse my concerns for strictly fair and equitable outcomes.

A Level Playing Field and Equal Opportunities

There is another way of thinking about this that concentrates not so much on the outcomes of resource distributions, but rather on the question of whether fair opportunity was in place to allow individuals to achieve these outcomes (Galston 1986; Jacobs 2004). A game analogy is often used to help think about the meaning of a fair opportunity. For instance, imagine two young children running a race. We can think about different types of situations in which this race might occur. Some situations may be clearly unfair, some may be clearly fair, and some may be somewhere in the middle.

Let's consider a situation where a child, child A, runs the race on a very flat field and another child, child B, runs the race up a steep hill. Naturally, child A wins, but we would not say this was fair. Clearly the playing field was so uneven that child A's win should not count. Now let's think about another situation. In this case child A starts a 100-yard race on the 50-yard line while child B starts the same race on the 1-yard line. Again, if child A wins, the win would be deemed unfair and should not count. These are the easy examples. Other easy examples would be if different rules were used to define what winning meant for child A and child B or what were game violations and requisite penalties for such violations. To be fair, both individuals should also be equally aware of game rules and these rules should be implemented with consistency and impartiality. This all seems straightforward.

But what if things get a little more complicated? For instance, what if child A's training or equipment is significantly better than child B's? What if the person in charge of this race is a relative of child A? What if child A's father actually wrote the rule book for this kind of race? What if child A is significantly stronger and taller than child B? Should these types of lack of equivalencies also count when judgments of winning and losing are made?

As we ask all these types of questions, we can try to think what we mean in our own mind when we state that we would like a "level playing field" to be in place. To be level does everything have to be exactly the same or is it enough to provide everyone with sufficient opportunity to play the game with some reasonable chance of success? Is it just the physical nature of the field that we are talking about, or do things that occurred off the field also have to be taken into consideration? Finally, are some of these factors more important at some ages than others?

Getting Us Off to a Good Start

It could be argued that in the early stages of life we are obligated to give people as much of an opportunity to learn and excel as possible, but that at some point this obligation diminishes. For instance, I may feel it is unfair if one group of 4-year-old children were given lots of resources and another group nothing at all, and then the first group was warmly praised for doing better on some task than the second group. However, if a similar situation occurred when these individuals were 40 or 50 years of age, I might have a different reaction. At this age, I might just say that is the way life is. Everything cannot be equal all the time. So it appears when we talk of a level playing field and equal opportunity, we may mean different things for groups of different ages.

What If "Fair Play" Leads to Uneven Outcomes?

Another consideration is how to evaluate the meaning of any outcome inequalities among individuals or groups that might occur even if we think the playing field has been sufficiently level. Does our "fair play" assessment free us from any concerns about outcome discrepancies? Should we particularly worry if discrepancies in outcomes among us become quite large, or if the absolute level of resources available to some groups has fallen to a particularly low point?

Some scholars such as Rawls (1971) argue that we should never endorse a standard of justice that has the most negative effect on the least advantaged among us. This is argued for several reasons. First, it is asserted that there are simply too many biases and built-in disparities in status and power in our social systems for everyone to have an adequate opportunity to achieve success in life. There are also many uncontrollable factors that negatively affect individuals' ability to pursue their goals and subtle patterns of discrimination that hold people back. Furthermore, aside from considerations of fair process, it is believed that all individuals simply have a right to a certain level of outcomes to assure their well-being and to protect them from indignity. This right is seen as being an absolute and not strictly earned. Thus, according to this perspective, in addition to granting everyone a chance at fair play in life, society should also feel obligated to provide people with a fair share of outcomes to guard against conditions such as extreme poverty, hunger, and sickness. Of course, we can agree in principle with this perspective, but still disagree with what a share of resources would be necessary in order to confer upon everyone a certain level of basic dignity.

Accumulation of Privilege Over Time

This becomes even more complicated as we look at the effect of privilege over time. Those espousing privilege theory (McIntosh 1989) suggest that privilege is systemic and cumulative in society. According to this viewpoint, certain groups favored by society tend to go through life with support systems and invisible assets that allow them to maneuver in life with greater ease than someone without these supports and assets. For instance, if I am white I may be able to do everyday things more easily than if I were a person of color. To name a few things, I can more easily get a cab to stop for me at night, I can go into the lobby of an expensive hotel and no one will bother me, and I can step into a bank without causing others to fear. Each of these things in and of themselves may be quite small but they serve to smooth my way through my day and open up possibilities for me. These sorts of privileges also tend to build up and up over generations. For instance, if I am very well off I may be able to provide my children with a very rich and privileged life. My children may go to expensive schools where they may meet and marry other children of rich families. These privileged couples then go on to have their own children and the cycle compounds over time. The degree of inequality between the haves and the have-nots continues to grow (Cassidy 2013).

Again the question arises of just how similar our range of opportunities has to be in order for the situation to be considered fair. Our thoughts about this have psychological and behavioral consequences. If we think the game is completely rigged and we have no chance of winning because of that, we probably will never even try out for "the team". Because of this we also will never learn the skills we would have learned by playing, or make the helpful acquaintances we would have made by being part of the team. On the other hand, if we completely ignore the fact that some aspects of the game are not equivalent for all players (for instance, I am climbing up a hill in my race and you are on a flat field), then if we lose we may engage in needless self-blame and self-deprecation. One answer is to strive for a better field, while still playing on the one that we have, but acknowledging that it is not perfect. This would allow us to continue playing the game, while trying to improve the conditions on which we play at the same time. This is often easier said than done.

How Do People React to Being Privileged?

Another question we can ask is how people respond to the idea that they themselves have privilege. If a person has more resources than most others, do they see this as being as unfair as if they had less? The answer is that sometimes they do. And sometimes this privileged situation makes people feel very uncomfortable. For instance, research has shown that if people are made aware that they are being grossly overpaid for doing some task, they often begin to feel very anxious and they may do a variety of things to try to correct this. They may, for example, work harder to justify their situation or attempt to compensate others more to make up for any perceived imbalance (Greenberg 1988). A very wealthy person might set up a foundation or a charitable institution that serves the interests of society in various ways. If the overcompensated situation feels too intolerable, people may even attempt to leave the situation entirely (Walster, Walster and Berscheid 1978). Furthermore, if fairness principles are made salient, altruistic motives can be evoked and individuals are more apt to work to help the disadvantaged even though it is against their own self-interests (Montada and Schneider 1989).

These types of findings offer some support for the idea that what people seek when they seek fairness and equity is not simply self-advantage, but a sense of proportionality. People apparently want to be fairly and appropriately rewarded, but not overcompensated, for their efforts. They want to earn what they receive in their own eyes and the eyes of the world. This, at least, is most individuals' aspiration. But sometimes making changes to reduce a sense of overcompensation is difficult. People may not want to leave a well-paid job or may not feel up to working harder or more strenuously. Particularly if the pattern of overcompensation persists for some time, subtle adjustments in perception may occur that allow individuals to feel more justified with their advantaged position. For instance, individuals may begin to inflate their perception of their own contributions, and to denigrate the worth of the contributions of others. Research, in fact, indicates that people use these types of privilege justification strategies quite often both to reduce any guilt they might have over their "undeserved" rewards or to lessen others' potential anger toward them for receiving such rewards (Chen and Tyler 2001; Jost, Banaji and Nosek 2004). Interestingly, in some situations people without privilege have also shown these privilege justification tendencies (Jost, Wakslak and Tyler 2008). Since they want to feel the world is just and fair (Lerner and Montada 1998), they may try to accomplish this by endorsing ideologies that denigrate the value of their own achievements (Jost, Pelham, Sheldon and Sullivan 2003). This may be particularly the case if individuals think that they cannot act to rectify their bad situation or do not want to upset a certain established order.

We also know that some people are more prone to self-aggrandizement than others. People who are high on what are called narcissistic personality traits, for instance, exhibit a greater sense of entitlement and a greater feeling that others owe them something in life than do people who score lower on this trait (Twenge and Campbell 2009). In addition to being related to genetic temperament, these narcissistic traits can be influenced by the situation one is in. For instance, children of parents who over praise them and tell them that they are unusually gifted and uniquely talented may begin to believe that they deserve more in life than others simply because they are "special" (Brown 2008). Also, people easily become used to any privileges they have. A movie star who used to wait on tables for a living may now feel that he or she deserves the very best seat in the very best restaurant in town. What was once a privilege now becomes a right.

All of the above suggests that while people may truly believe that they want to receive only their fair share from others in life and nothing more, the way fair share is defined is not straightforward. Sometimes people are so uncomfortable with the notion of privilege that they may simply deny that it exists in society. To admit that many times outcomes are unearned both for ourselves and others might seem to violate the whole premise that the world we live in is fair. Thus, we may not feel uncomfortable asserting that certain people are fortunate in life, but we may squirm a bit at the notion of some having more privilege than others.

What's Luck Got to Do With It?

Thinking About Good Luck

We have been discussing the idea of a just distribution of resources in society. Now we are going to examine the nature of luck and consider how or if we should factor luck into equations of deservingness. Estimates vary, but we know that luck plays a considerable role in our success or lack of success in life (Gladwell 2011; Thompson 2014). For instance, perhaps I met my future husband because by chance I was standing behind him in line for a movie. Perhaps I received a good grade on a test because, by chance, I studied information about the two questions that were asked on the test. All of these are to some degree examples of achievement by luck. Something happenstance occurred and I gained some reward from it. To consider this a bit more, think about the following possible sequence of events. Imagine that you obtained a big part in a play because the star actress came down with the flu the night before they were casting her role. Without the star actress getting sick you never would have gotten the part in the play. Without getting the part in this first play, you never would have been noticed and then cast for another larger role in a second bigger play. And, finally, without being in this second play, which was a big hit, you never would have been given worldwide acclaim and been recognized as a major movie star in your own right. Did you earn your stardom? Do you deserve it? Do you deserve it more than people who had as much talent and worked just as hard but never had a lucky break that put them in the right place at the right point in time? These are hard questions.

Is Bad Luck My Fault?

We can also look at luck from the vantage point of bad luck. Imagine, for instance, that a person developed some kind of cancer in part because they had the bad luck of being born with a certain type of gene that predisposes one to cancer. Is this case more unfair that someone who developed lung cancer because they smoked two packs of cigarette a day for 30 years? That is, does attributing something to luck lessen the blame we should place on victims of bad fortune? Should we feel as sorry for one person as the other? Should society agree to pay the costs of health care as readily for one person as the other?

People have different views about when and why people should be protected from misfortune. A simple idea that has been discussed is what is called luck equalitarian (Dworkin 1981; Sher 2010). Here the notion is that if a person brought the bad luck on his or herself by risky behavior or thoughtless decisions, society should not be particularly obligated to aid the individual if and when harm to them occurs. If, however, misfortune was due to some uncontrollable factors such as genetic inheritance, then societies' duty to assist the person in their misfortune may be stronger. The problem with this idea is that in many cases blame or responsibility for misfortune cannot be so easily determined. Oftentimes, in fact, numerous factors interact in complex ways to produce a particular event, and untangling single causation is difficult. There may also be some situations in which misfortune is so severe that even if the harmed individual was clearly at fault, it is seen as unjust not to assist them. As an example of this, we would aid a person whose house was burning down even though the fire occurred because that person was smoking in bed.

Are Some People Just Born Lucky?

We have been discussing random situational occurrences that result in good or bad outcomes for individuals. But what if some people seem more prone to good or bad luck than others in their life? Is that fair? This question has, in fact, been the subject of some research. What research suggests is that while some individuals may, in fact, be more or less lucky than others, sometimes people create their own luck. They do this by recognizing and capitalizing on chance occurrences and creating positive opportunities out of seemingly random events (Wiseman 2003). That is, if by chance in a parking lot I meet the producer of a movie I am trying out for, I first take advantage of this opportunity to promote myself and then, if I eventually get the part, I use this to open up pathways to other positive experiences. I take credit for my good fortune and define myself as lucky at the same time. There is a self-fulfilling prophesy to all of this as well. For instance, if I expect to be lucky, I may be more motivated to scan for opportunities in the future in which my continued good fortune will be revealed. If I expect to be unlucky, I may be a bit less eager to engage in this kind of quest.

Of course, belief in luck can cut another way as well. If we believe too strongly that most outcomes in life are due to sheer random luck, our incentive to work hard to achieve our goals through our own effort could become diminished. After all, if luck is the only determinate of success, why bother to try? Fairness, also, has no real meaning here because whatever occurs is simply the result of chance.

Special Cases of Deservingness

So far we have examined the ideas of deservingness, privilege, and the concept of fairly or unfairly earning the rewards one receives in life. In this last section on distributive justice, we will look at whether there are special cases of deservingness that require our particular attention.

We have already mentioned that many writers think that children deserve special consideration when we think of what is fair or not fair. Since children are just starting in life, it may be especially important that they all receive an equal opportunity to grow and develop and to learn. Of course, we all know that this is often not the case and the question becomes how much inequality or lack of fair play we can tolerate among children before we define the societal system in which they live as unfair. Where this tipping point is, naturally, is often a very subjective call.

We can also ask whether certain vulnerable groups in society such as the very elderly or those who have debilitating mental or physical conditions that interfere with their ability to fully participate in society deserve special consideration. Most individuals would probably say that they do.

In addition, we can examine not who should receive dispensations or special support, but rather who among us should be singled out for unique rewards. Are there people in our society who fulfill certain types of roles that merit special consideration? We might suggest, for instance, that people who put their life on the line for us such as the police or military personnel deserve some kind of special praise. Or, perhaps, those who heal or those who teach or those who build bridges or start business and add jobs to our economy should be seen as especially deserving. The idea here is that most resources should go to those who benefit society most. As we think about this we can see that we end this discussion at the same place that we began. What is merit? How should the worth and benefit to society be judged? Is fairness even a relevant concept to use when evaluating the justice of our market-based system?

Case Studies for Further Inquiry: Privilege and Luck

Privileged Hiring

This case concerns the question of fairness in hiring decisions. Imagine the following.

> *A young man named Jacob received a big position in a company that his father owned. Jacob was hired by his father for this position over many other more qualified and experienced applicants. Jacob just graduated from college and he is his father's only son.*

1. Is the decision to hire Jacob fair?
2. What other questions would you need to ask before you could decide this?
3. Does the fact that Jacob was hired over many other more strictly qualified applicants make a difference in how you think about this?
4. Should Jacob feel obligated to work particularly hard in his new position to justify his selection?
5. What if Jacob's father did not hire his son for this job, but rather, as a favor to Jacob, hired Jacob's friend who also was less qualified than many other applicants. Would this be less fair than hiring Jacob?

Opportunity Privilege

Here we look at another question about the fairness of opportunity privilege. Imagine the following.

> *A woman named Jessica made lots of money as an internationally famous artist. Because of the money she acquired from selling her artwork, Jessica was able to provide many material resources to her children. Her children were able to go to some of the finest prep schools in the country and to attend college at some of the most elite institutions in the United States. They traveled the world with their mother and had many tutors and mentors who helped them achieve their goals in life.*

1. Should the type of privilege that Jessica was able to give to her children be considered differently than the kind of privilege depicted in the previous case where a father hired his son?
2. Should Jessica's children feel uneasy because they did not directly earn their privileged status by dint of their own work?
3. Should Jessica's children feel guilty or compelled to work harder than some of their peers who are less privileged in order to justify their good fortune?
4. Would it make any difference if you knew that Jessica herself had worked 18-hour days for many years in order to provide the best for her children and to achieve success as an artist?

Being Underprivileged and Having Bad Luck

In this case, we examine how we should think about the fairness of loss of privilege. Imagine the following.

> *Two individuals were recently fired from a good paying job because of poor job performance. The first individual named Emma was born with a certain subtle neural disability that makes it difficult for her to process information quickly. Because of her condition, Emma has been increasingly unable to keep up with the demands of her job. She tires easily and has difficulty concentrating for sustained periods of time. The second individual, Edward, came from a very underprivileged background. He attended very poor quality schools and was raised in a very chaotic family environment. This background made it challenging for Edward to acquire the skills necessary to do well in his high pressured job. Edward often could not keep pace with his colleagues and he tended to make many errors in his work.*

1. Was it fair to fire Emma?
2. What if Emma had had a more visible disability that interfered with her work such as blindness or deafness? Would it be more unfair to fire her then?
3. What if Emma had a psychological disability such as depression?

4. Was it fair to fire Edward?

5. What if we knew that Edward was the first one to graduate from high school in his family and the first to take some post high school training classes to increase his job skills? Should Edward's efforts to improve himself be factored at all in the decision to fire him?

Why Is This All Important?

A much debated question is why a sense of distributive fairness is important to us at all. We know that people often use the word "fair" to justify their resource demands. What does that mean, though? If I say I feel deprived and that it is not fair that I have less than you, how can we tell whether this stems from my selfish desire to get more for myself or if it truly reflects my concern with some abstract principle of justice? Sometimes that is hard to tell because self-interest assertions can be confounded with our apparent justice interests. We do know that young children do not even try to hide their selfish motives. For instance, if I give a young child a big piece of cake and her friend a much smaller piece of cake, the child with the smaller piece will simply demand to have more of what her friend has. No pretense of higher principles here. But with adults, it is trickier. We sometimes may be motivated to mask blatant self-interest behind a façade of more socially acceptable attitudes. I may say, for example, that I am only concerned with what is fair when I am really concerned with simply getting more of what I want.

There is also a societal component to this. If all of us simply strive to maximize ourselves and satisfy our own desires, society would be a very difficult place in which to live. Everyone would be constantly battling and fighting over resources to find an advantage for themselves. This would lead to a very unstable situation. Thus, in order to cooperate with others and learn to function effectively as a society, we agree on certain moral principles that guide our behavior and certain rules that define how these principles should be put into effect. We learn to compromise and to give up the idea of perfect "fairness" for every interaction in which we engage in order to promote the smooth functioning of day-to-day life (Lerner and Clayton 2011; Tyler 2011). One thing that helps us do this is to switch from short-term thinking about fairness to more long-term thinking (Hafer, Begue, Choma and Dempsey 2005). Here we might say to ourselves that today I might not always receive what is fair (or what I want), but over time in the long run I will be rewarded appropriately and will get what I deserve. Furthermore, the same will be true for others. This type of thinking, then, allows me to believe in a fair world in a general sense, but still make the accommodations necessary to function effectively and efficiently in society. Of course, my tendency to think about "what I deserve" may be a little biased, and I may conflate my sense of my own contributions and denigrate others in order to justify fulfillment of my own desires (Lerner and Montada 1998).

The above paints a somewhat cynical analysis of our quest for fairness. In this view, fairness concerns are simply masked instrumental self-interest. Here, fairness, at best, serves to promote a system of mutually beneficial social exchange (Deutsch 1975). Other scholars such as Montada (2002) and Ratner and Miller (2001) strongly disagree with these narrow self-interest interpretations. They assert that people seem quite capable, at times, of sacrificing their own interests to enhance the outcomes of others. There may be individual differences, however, in this tendency to focus on others versus the self, and in the extent to which people react negatively to perceived personal injustices (Van Lange 1999; Schmitt, Baumert, Gollwitzer and Maes 2010). In general, how we are treated by others can serve as an indication to us about how much we are valued or esteemed in our society. This could be either as an individual or as a member of the groups to which we belong. Thus, if I receive more resources than you this means my contributions have been found to be particularly worthy. At its core, this viewpoint suggests that concerns about justice are linked in some ways with concerns about identity. We will say more about this view when we discuss procedural justice in Chapter 2.

Applications: Putting This Together to Debate Some Bigger Policy Issues

We have reviewed some of the major research and theories of distributive justice and thought about some situations where fairness is ambiguous. Now you will be given the opportunity to use these ideas as a framework to critically analyze some of the important distributive justice policy questions of our times. We know that at the present moment in our culture a great disparity exists in terms of how resources are distributed among individuals. The top 1 percent owns half of the resources in the world (Bentley 2015). This reflects a degree of inequality among people that is at record levels. This inequality varies by type of resource. For instance, the results when we look at income may be different than the results for something like health care services or educational opportunities. How should income be distributed in society? Who should and should not have access to health care resources and why? What types of standards should we use to allocate educational opportunities to children in society?

In the following section, ideas and proposals pertaining to each of these issues will be presented. After each proposal, a series of questions will be asked. There are no right or wrong answers to these questions. Rather they are presented to spark thinking and debate.

Major Allocation Dilemma #1: "The Death Tax"

There has been much debate about the fairness of taxing individual's estates after they die. Proponents of not taxing these estates argue that the individuals involved earned whatever they have and should have the right to pass it on to whomever they want as a kind of legacy. Proponents of taxing these estates, on the other hand, suggest that the inheritors of these estates did nothing in their own right to deserve what will be passed on to them. According to this view, the inheritance is not justified because it is not the result of the inheritors' own merit.

Construct arguments in support of both sides of this issue. What position seems most fair to you in an ideal world? Why?

Other points to ponder in terms of fairness:

1. Should the size of any income disparity among individuals that might result if the plan that you endorsed was enacted be taken into consideration as you think about what is fair?
2. In one's will, is it fairer to give tax-free estates to charity rather than to give a tax-free inheritance to one's family? Why?

3. Should how an individual earned his or her money be taken into account when one thinks of the fairness of taxing or not taxing inheritance? For instance, should a person who made his money running brothels in Nevada have the same right to leave a tax-free financial legacy as another who helped the underprivileged all her life? Why or why not?

Major Allocation Dilemma #2: Health Care Resources

Another major question we must face as a society is how to fairly allocate health care resources to others. The key question here is whether access to health care should be considered a right or a privilege. If we think of health care as a right, we would say that *all* individuals are entitled to health care when they need it. If we think of health care as a privilege we would say that individuals should be given health care only if they have earned enough money to pay for these services through their own past work, effort, and savings.

Construct arguments in support of both sides of this issue. What position seems most fair to you in an ideal world? Why?

Other points to ponder in terms of fairness:

1. Should the age of the health care recipient make a difference? That is, is it fair that a 90-year-old receives the same level of services as a 24-year-old in a similar condition (e.g., needing a heart transplant)?
2. Should the type of contribution an individual makes to society figure in health care access decision making? Imagine, for example, that two people are awaiting a kidney transplant and that kidneys are in short supply. Should a brilliant scientist who is adding to our knowledge of how to cure cancer receive the same level of health care resources as a person with a history of violence and antisocial behavior? Why or why not?
3. Would it make a difference to your position if you knew that many people requesting health care services have contributed in some way to the onset of their own illness? For instance, many may be sick because they have eaten too much food and became overweight, smoked too many cigarettes, drank too much alcohol, or exercised too infrequently. Is it fair to take these types of factors into consideration?

Major Allocation Dilemma #3: Access to Educational Opportunities

For a final allocation dilemma to consider for this chapter, think about who should have access to the highest quality educational opportunities. Imagine that in this country several elite model educational institutions have been built. The best teachers are recruited to teach at these schools and each classroom is equipped with the best state-of-the-art educational resources. Students from all over the country have been screened for admission into these schools, and those who are selected have to meet rigorous admission standards. Now each school has some extra money to give out to a particularly "deserving" student who has met the admission requirements. The question that the school administrators have to decide is what does "deserving" mean in this context.

Two different proposals are offered. In the first proposal, it is suggested that that the child who scores the highest on tests of academic ability should receive the award money. In a second proposal, it is suggested that child who comes from the most deprived and challenging social and economic background should, instead, be given the money.

Construct arguments in support of both sides of this issue. Which position seems most fair to you in an ideal world? Why?

Other points to ponder in terms of fairness:

1. Should the age of the child be taken into consideration as you think about to whom the award money should be given? That is, should decisions about these awards be made in the same way for very young children as they are for older children or young adults?
2. Is it fair to give special consideration to individuals who come from groups who have been historically under-represented in the past at these types of elite educational institutions? That is, should we take into account not just the child's present circumstances, but also the historical educational legacy of his or her group?
3. Should the children of parents who are alumni of these schools be given special consideration for these awards? That is should so-called legacy children be granted special privileges.

Summary

In this chapter a review of the major research findings in the area of distributive justice was presented. Distributive justice concerns how to fairly allocate resources in society, or determinations of who should have what, when, and where. Besides addressing these basic questions, special attention was given to a consideration of the justice of inequalities in resources among individuals and the meaning of the concept of deservingness.

Several key themes emerged from the literature review on distributive justice. First, determinations of distributive justice are, for the most part, comparative and perceptions of unfairness resulting from perceptions of deprivation are relative. This deprivation can occur at the individual or group level, and each of these forms of deprivation is associated with different emotional responses and action tendencies. Second, various standards are used by individuals to determine whether allocations are fair or unfair, but the three most commonly employed standards are merit, need, and equality. Each of these facilitates different justice goals and promotes different sorts of relationships among individuals.

In addition to studying reactions to deprivation, researchers have also examined the nature of privilege. Privilege, too, is a relative concept and consists of both the possession of material things and access to opportunities, power, and influence. Privilege may be subtle and often unacknowledged by the possessor of it. Although individuals can experience discomfort with having overly large discrepancies of outcomes between themselves and others, they can also learn to psychologically defend such discrepancies by employing a variety of privilege justification strategies. Many more facets of distributive justice have been researched, and they can be found in Jasso, Törnblom, and Sabbagh (2016).

References

Adams, J. Stacey. 1965. "Injustice in Social Exchange." *Advances in Experimental Social Psychology.* 2: 267–299.

Barrett-Howard, Edith and Tom Tyler. 1986. "Perceptions of Justice as a Criterion in Allocation Decisions." *Journal of Personality and Social Psychology.* 50 (2): 296–304.

Bentley, Daniel. 2015. "The Top 1% Now Own Half the World's Wealth." *Fortune*, October 14th.

Brown, Nina W. 2008. *Children of the Self-Absorbed: A Grown-ups Guide to Getting Over Narcissistic Parents* (2nd edition). Oakland, CA: New Harbinger Press.

Buechler, Steven M. 2016. *Understanding Social Movements*. New York, NY: Routledge Press.

Buttram, Robert, T., Robert Folger and B.H. Sheppard. 1995. "Equity, Equality and Need: Three Faces of Social Justice." In *Conflict, Cooperation and Justice: Essays Inspired by the Work of Morton Deutsch*, edited by Morton Deutsch, Jeffrey Rubin and Barbara B. Bunker, 261–289, San Francisco, CA: Jossey-Bass Inc.

Cassidy, John. 2013. "American Inequality in Six Charts." *The New Yorker*, November 18.

Chen, Emmeline and Tom Tyler. 2001. "Cloaking Power: Legitimizing Myths and the Psychology of the Disadvantaged." In *The Use and Abuse of Power*, edited by John A. Barch and A.Y. Lee-Chai. New York, NY: Psychology Press.

Crosby, Faye. 1976. "A Model of Egotistical Relative Deprivation." *Psychological Review*. 83 (2): 85–113.

Crosby, Faye. 1982. *Relative Deprivation and Working Women*. Oxford, England: Oxford University Press.

Deutsch, Morton. 1975. "Equity, Equality and Need: What Determines Which Value Will Be Used as a Basis for Distributive Justice?" *Journal of Social Issues*. 31: 137–149.

Deutsch, Morton. 1985. *Distributive Justice*. New Haven, CT: Yale University Press.

Dworkin, Ronald. 1981. "What Is Equality? Part 2: Equality of Resources." *Philosophy and Public Affairs*. 10 (4): 283–345.

Galston, William. 1986. "Equality of Opportunity and Liberal Theory." In *Justice and Equality Here and Now*, edited by Frank S. Lucash and Judith N. Shklar, 89–107. Ithaca, NY: Cornell University Press.

Gladwell, Malcolm. 2011. *Outliers: The Story of Success*. Boston, MA: Back Bay Books.

Greenberg, Jerald. 1988. "Equity and Workplace Status: A Field Experiment." *Journal of Applied Psychology*. 73: 606–613.

Hafer, Carolyn, Laurent Begue, Becky Choma and Julie Dempsey. 2005. "Belief in a Just World and Commitment to Long-term Deserved Outcomes". *Social Justice Research*. 18 (4): 429–444.

Haslam, Nick. 2015. "Dehumanization and Intergroup Relations." In *APA Handbook of Personality and Social Psychology*, edited by Mario Mikulincer and Philip R. Shaver, 295–314, Washington, DC: APA Press.

Huo, Yuen J. 2002. "Justice and the Regulation of Social Relations: When and Why Do Group Members Deny Claims to Social Goods?" *British Journal of Social Psychology*. 41: 535–562.

Jacobs, Lesley A. 2004. *Pursuing Equal Opportunities*. Cambridge, England: Cambridge University Press.

Jasso, Guillermina, Kjell Y. Törnblom and Clara Sabbagh. 2016. "Distributive Justice." In *The Handbook of Social Justice Theory and Research*, edited by Clara Sabbagh and Manfred Schmitt, 210–218, New York, NY: Springer

Jost, John T., Brett W. Pelham, Oliver Sheldon and Bilian Ni Sullivan. 2003. "Social Inequality and the Reduction of Ideological Dissonance on Behalf of the System: Evidence of Enhanced System Justification Among the Disadvantaged." *European Journal of Social Psychology*. 33: 13–36.

Jost, John T., Mahzarin R. Banaji and Brian A. Nosek. 2004. "A Decade of System Justification Theory: Accumulated Evidence of Conscious and Unconscious Bolstering of the Status Quo." *Political Psychology*. 25 (6): 881–919.

Jost, John T., Cheryl Wakslak and Tom Tyler. 2008. "System Justification Theory and the Alleviation of Emotional Distress: Palliative Effects of Ideology in an Arbitrary Social Hierarchy and in Society." *Advances in Group Processes*. 25: 181–211.

Knight, Carl and Zofia Stemplowski, eds. 2011. *Responsibility and Distributive Justice*. Oxford, England: Oxford University Press.

Laham, Simon M. 2009. "Expanding the Moral Circle: Inclusion and Exclusion Mindsets and the Circle of Moral Regard." *Journal of Experimental Social Psychology*. 45: 250–253.

Lamont, Julian. 1994. "The Concept of Desert in Distributive Justice." *The Philosophical Quarterly*. 44 (174): 45–64.

Lerner, Melvin J. and Leo Montada. 1998. "Responses to Victimization and Belief in a Just Word." In *An Overview: Advances in Belief in a*

Just World Theory and Methods, edited by Leo Montada and Melvin J. Lerner, 1–7. New York, NY: Springer Publishing.

Lerner, Melvin J. and Susan Clayton. 2011. *Justice and Self-interest: Two Fundamental Motives.* Cambridge, England: Cambridge University Press.

Masters, John C. and William P. Smith. 1987. *Social Comparison, Social Justice and Relative Deprivation.* Hillsdale, NJ: Lawrence Erlbaum Associates.

McIntosh, Peggy. 1989. "White Privilege: Unpacking the Invisible Knapsack". *Peace and Freedom Magazine,* July/August, 10–12.

Milne, Heather. 1986. "Desert, Effort and Equality." *Journal of Applied Philosophy.* 3 (2): 235–243.

Montada, Leo. 2002. "Justice to the Justice Motive." In *The Justice Motive in Everyday Life,* edited by Michael Ross and Dale T. Miller, 44–62, New York, NY: Cambridge University Press.

Montada, Leo and Angela Schneider. 1989. "Justice and Emotional Reactions to the Disadvantaged." *Social Justice Research.* 8 (4): 73–90.

Olson, James M., C. Peter Herman and Mark P. Zanna, eds. 1986. *Relative Deprivation and Social Comparison.* Hillsdale, NJ: Lawrence Erlbaum Associates.

Opotow, Susan. 1990. "Moral Exclusion and Injustice: An Introduction." *Journal of Social Issues.* 46 (1): 1–20.

Ratner, Rebecca and Dale T. Miller. 2001. "The Norm of Self-Interest and Its Effect on Social Action." *Journal of Personality and Social Psychology.* 81: 5–16.

Rawls, John. 1971. *A Theory of Justice.* Cambridge, MA: Harvard University Press.

Reed, Americus and Karl F. Aquino. 2003. "Moral Identity and the Circle of Moral Regard Towards Out-groups." *Journal of Personality and Social Psychology.* 84: 1270–1286.

Ross, Jerry D. 1982. *Outbreaks, the Sociology of Collective Behavior.* New York, NY: New York Free Press.

Runciman, William G. 1966. *Relative Deprivation and Social Justice.* Berkeley, CA: University of California Press.

Sadurski, Wojciech. 1985. *Giving Desert Its Due.* New York, NY: Springer Publishing.

Schmitt, Manfred, Anna Baumert, Mario Gollwitzer and Jürgen Maes. 2010. "The Justice Sensitivity Inventory: Factorial Validity, Location in the Personality Facet Space, Demographic Pattern, and Normative Data." *Social Justice Research*. 23: 211–238.

Sher, George. 2010. "Real-World Luck Equalitarianism." *Social Philosophy and Policy.* 27 (1): 218–232.

Smith, Heather, Thomas Pettigrew, Gina Pippin and Silvana Bialosiewicz. 2012. "Relative Deprivation: A Theoretical and Meta-analytical Review." *Personality and Social Psychology Review*. 16: 203–232.

Smith, Heather and Tom Pettigrew. 2014. "The Subjective Interpretation of Inequality: A Model of the Relative Deprivation Experience." *Social and Personality Psychology Compass*. 8 (12): 755–765.

Thompson, N. Taylor. 2014. "Life is Luck: Here's How to Plan a Career Around It". *Harvard Business Review*, January.

Twenge, Jean J. and W. Keith Campbell. 2009. *The Narcissism Epidemic: Living in an Age of Entitlement*. New York, NY: Free Press.

Tyler, Tom. 2011. *Why People Cooperate: The Role of Social Motivations*. Princeton, NJ: Princeton University Press.

Van Lange, Paul. 1999. "The Pursuit of Joint Outcomes and Equality in Outcomes: An Integrative Model of Social Value Orientation." *Journal of Personality and Social Psychology*. 77: 337–349.

Van Zomeren, Marijn, Tom Postmes and Russell Spears. 2008. "Toward an Integrative Social Identity Model of Collective Action: A Qualitative Research Synthesis of Three Socio-psychological Perspectives." *Psychological Bulletin*. 134: 504–535.

Walster, Elaine, G. William Walster and Ellen S. Berscheid. 1978. *Equity Theory and Research*. Boston, MA: Allen and Bacon.

Wiseman, Richard. 2003. "The Luck Factor." *Skeptical Inquirer, May/ June 1–5.*

CHAPTER 2

Procedural Justice

Abstract

In this chapter the topic of procedural justice is discussed. Procedural justice refers to the fairness of the processes or procedures we use to make decisions. It answers the question of how we were treated rather than what we received. Several aspects of procedures have been found to affect these types of fairness judgments, including our perceptions that we were allowed to have sufficient input or "voice" in the decision-making process. We also tend to find procedures fairer if, among other things, they are consistent over person and place and if they are employed without evidence of decision-maker bias. Being treated with dignity is also hugely important to us in our fairness evaluations.

Major headings within this chapter include participatory justice and the effect of having voice, the rules of the game, and interactional justice. Each of these major chapter sections is further divided into several subsections.

Definition of Procedural Justice

In the previous chapter we examined the concept of distributive justice and talked about why it is important to individuals. As we discussed, distributive justice concerns considerations of how we should fairly allocate resources in society. It answers questions such as "Did I obtain my fair share?" and "Did I get what I deserve?" In this chapter we will shift our perspective. Rather than looking at how we determine if the outcomes we receive from others are fair, we will concentrate on the process leading to those outcomes. We will examine such questions as "Was I treated fairly?" and "Were the procedures that were used to make decisions just?" As we shall see, our perceptions of how fairly we were treated by others turn out to be as important to us in many cases as our assessments of the justness of the outcomes we received.

Participatory Justice: The Effect of Having Voice

What Is Voice?

To start our discussion of procedural justice, we might imagine the following. Think about two individuals who have worked for a similar period of time for a certain company and who are now being considered for a promotion. Each individual has different skills and brings a different quality and style to their work. Imagine a first case in which a company boss simply unilaterally decides to promote one worker and not to promote the other. Naturally, from a distributive justice point of view, the worker who received the less personally favorable outcome would be likely to define the decision as being less fair than the worker who received the more favorable outcome. This would seem to be a straightforward prediction. But we can imagine another scenario. In this version, the boss similarly retains her decision-making authority, but before her decision is made she invites both workers to present their case as to why each should deserve the raise. Each worker can talk about what talents they uniquely bring to their jobs and why what they contribute is valuable to the company. They can ask questions of the boss and seek clarification of the boss's opinion. After this process, the boss takes into account what each individual has said and then makes her promotion decision.

Research has shown that in the second scenario the worker who was *not* given the promotion is more likely to be happier with the boss's decision than in the first scenario. This is because we feel better about decision-making processes if we think we were listened to and given the opportunity to represent our version of events. Having our say in these kinds of situations has been referred to as having "voice" (Folger, Rosenfield, Grove and Corkran 1979; Lind and Tyler 1988). We will talk more later about why having this type of voice is so important to us, but the point to remember for now is that what happens to us in a bottom-line sense is not the only thing we care about. Rather, we are also very sensitive to how decisions about us are made.

At first glance, the above ideas may seem obvious. Of course, we like to be treated in a manner that acknowledges our ideas and views. But this is actually a nonintuitive finding, and it seems to be somewhat unique to humans. For instance, we would not expect that a lioness who is searching for food for her cubs would spend time thinking about whether the fight for food was fair or whether she could make her opinions known about what food she thinks she deserves. This would seem absurd, and in her fight for survival we would expect her to care only about the outcome of her search, not about how this outcome was achieved. We, as humans, however, seem to view things differently in the sense that we are concerned with both fair outcomes and fair processes. And we do not just say we care about fair process, but we actually feel and behave differently when we think such processes are in place. This, as we shall see, has remarkable and important consequences.

When Are Voice Effects Found?

Thibaut and Walker (1975) were some of the first researchers to document these powerful fair process effects. In much of this early work, justice perceptions were looked at in the context of a variety of legal proceedings. When, for example, would litigants in legal proceedings be most likely to accept legal rulings and when would they not? Was outcome favorability the only predictor of this? Did the process matter? Researchers demonstrated again and again that process did indeed matter. If people felt they had an opportunity to be heard and well represented in legal procedures, they would not only think the procedures were fairer, but they would also be more satisfied with legal rulings and more likely to comply with them (Lind and Tyler 1988; Tyler 1988).

These types of effects have been found in a variety of other settings and contexts, as well. For instance, researchers in what has been called organizational justice found that if individuals have a chance to have input into decision-making processes, they may be more willing to accept their bosses' views concerning salary recommendations, they may put up more graciously with firing decisions, they may comply and be satisfied with a variety of other workplace policies, and they may feel more generally committed to their organizations (Colquitt, Conlon, Wesson, Porter and Ng 2001; Cropanzano and Greenberg 1997; Van Prooijen 2009).

Voice effects have been noted across many cultures, although there is some research to suggest that they are particularly strong in more individualistic and egalitarian Western settings where the ability to freely express oneself in a nonhierarchical context is especially valued (Choi 2003).

Salience of Voice Effects

Although having a chance to have a voice in proceedings can have a huge impact on how we view such proceedings, there are certain circumstances in which these types of effects may be less strong. One example is when we are involved in a conflict with another in which any degree of agreement between us is simply unattainable because we are framing the issue in terms of standards of absolute rightness or wrongness rather than degree of fairness (Thibaut and Walker 1975). To think about this, we might imagine a situation in which a divorced couple was in court in order to have a decision made concerning the custody of their children. Perhaps the former wife thinks that the only possible solution would be for her to be granted complete custody because she feels she is the sole competent parent while the former husband thinks just the opposite. In this kind of circumstance, having had an opportunity for "voice" would not be expected to make a negative custody decision more palatable to either party. That would simply be superfluous to them.

In addition, for voice to be effective, it has to be implemented in a real way. That is, the person who is expressing themselves has to really think he or she is being heard. When you ask me to tell my side of the story, you cannot then start talking to someone else or begin to check your cell phone. This would clearly be a kind of sham voice opportunity. I have to trust your motives as a decision maker, as well, and think that you value the input I am giving (Bies 1986; Potter 2006).

The kind of relationship we have with another also affects the salience of voice effects. I will care more about being treated fairly by perceived ingroup than outgroup members (Van Prooijen, Van den Bos and Wilke 2004). In general, I also will be more likely to care about fair process issues if I am invested in seeing you again in the future, and if I anticipate that we will have productive social exchanges (Deutsch 1982). In such a case, it may be helpful for me to know that we will probably deal with each other fairly and politely. This expectation will ease our interactions with each other and generate a kind of bond between us. Such bond building may be less important if I know that our interactions will be very time limited, in which case selfish bottom-line outcome concerns would more likely take precedence (Rusbult and Van Lange 1996).

Voice, Trust Building, and Legitimacy

Even though the strength of voice effects varies across some situations, in general, these effects have been found to be remarkably robust. The fact that we care about voice and fair process independent of fair outcomes is hugely important because it paves the way for a potential type of social harmony that would not be possible if voice and process were not so central to us. For example, if receiving favorable outcomes was the only thing that mattered to us, we would only be satisfied with situations in which our own narrow self-interests were promoted. Every dispute among individuals would be a win-lose circumstance with each person needing to fight to get as much as possible for him- or herself. This would clearly be a tiring and untenable way to live. If, however, we could learn to sometimes trust others to make decisions for us, we could give up some of this need for constant battle. At its core, trust involves a kind of relinquishing of the need for control over another. Before we relinquish this control, though, we want some evidence that others will not take advantage of us and turn our trust into a farce. One thing we can use to help us judge this is our considerations of our previous experiences. Have you treated me fairly in the past? Has there been a process in place that allowed me to have input and express my opinions to you? Were you willing to listen to me? If the answer to these questions is yes, I can use this information as a kind of shortcut heuristic to manage any uncertainty I might have about our relationship and to predict that my trust in you will not be misplaced (Van den Bos and Lind 2002). This ability to let go and build trust is essential for without it we could not have a functioning society or a sense of legitimacy in our institutions (Tyler 2002). We will talk more about this in the following section of this chapter. For now we can simply state that establishing trust and valuing procedural as well as distributive justice have big social benefits.

The Rules of the Game

We have talked of the importance of being heard in our determinations of fair treatment. But there are other factors that we use to define fair treatment, as well. Let's look more closely at the structure of the decision-making process itself.

To think about this, we might imagine that we are playing some team sport. We have Team A and Team B. The referee blows his whistle and says that some kind of rule violation has occurred. Members of Team A agree and members of Team B disagree. The referee is called upon to make a decision about how to resolve this. Each side or team, of course, thinks they are right and the other side is wrong. How would we define "fair process" in this situation? Leventhal (1980) suggests six factors would be important to us as we think about this.

Procedural Consistency

First, we want procedures used to be consistent over time and people. For example, if I have played a certain game before and a similar violation occurred, I would want the referee to be consistent in what he or she called a foul then and a foul now. If it was a foul on Tuesday it should also be a foul on Wednesday. Also, I want consistency over individuals. That is, if I saw Peter commit a similar act and saw that it was not ruled a foul, I would want the same standard to apply to me.

Bias Suppression

Second, I want the referee to be neutral and to have no vested interest in any particular outcome. For example, if the referee's son Seth was playing in the game, and I noticed that Seth was never called for rule violations even though the fouls he committed again and again looked blatant to me, I might conclude that the referee was not being objective. It appeared that he had a vested interest in his son doing well. In that case, I would be less apt to accept the referee's decision.

Accuracy

Third, I want some proof that the referee's decisions were based on accurate information. Perhaps I noticed that the referee was making a decision on the basis of an account given by someone who had no background in this particular game. In this case, I might not trust the integrity of this decision-making process.

Correctability

I would also want some way of remedying inaccurate or misguided decisions. I would want, that is, to be able to say, "Look, that referee who gave you his account could not even see the players when the so-called rule violation was called. Let's examine something else such as a video replay or another referee's opinion." In this way I could correct the input used to make the decision and my perceptions of the fairness of the process would be enhanced.

Ethicality

Another thing I would look for is that the referee's decision conformed to basic ethical standards of behavior. For instance, if I found out that a certain referee had been paid off for making various kinds of game calls, I would want this person removed from his position, rather than allowing him to stay and undermine the integrity of the game.

Representativeness

Finally, I would want players who are from different sides to have the chance to voice their opinions about game calls. This would reduce the chance that one team's biases would unevenly and detrimentally influence final game results.

These elements are the structural factors we use to decide if decisions are fairly made or not. They serve, in a sense, as the glue that allows us to work with each other without constantly resorting to violence and coercion. When in place, they enable us to continue "playing the game."

Case Studies for Further Inquiry: Having Voice and Rule Fairness

A Traffic Ticket: What Is Fair?

To think about some of the above issues a bit more, consider the next few hypothetical cases. The first case concerns fairness in a common type of legal violation. Imagine the following.

> *A municipality in the United States is trying to decide on fair procedures for giving out traffic tickets in their town. In one plan, cameras would be installed at various sites in the town that would monitor motorists' speed and driving behavior. Anyone who was caught speeding on camera or engaging in any other type of traffic violation would be sent a traffic ticket in the mail. The motorist would be required to pay the ticket in 1 week or risk an even higher fine. There would be no appeal process.*
>
> *In a second proposal, traffic police would be placed throughout the city in unmarked cars at various locations. If a motorist was caught apparently speeding or violating some other type of traffic rule, the police officer would have the option of stopping the motorist. He or she would then ask the motorist to show car identification papers and to explain why they were speeding or engaging in some other type of rule violation. Based on the evidence obtained, the police officer could either let the motorist go, issue them a warning, or give them a traffic ticket. If the motorist disagreed with the ticket, they could present their case later before a traffic judge and he or she would render a decision about their situation.*

The municipality is trying to decide what plan to put in place. They want a process that people perceive as being fair, that they comply with, and that will enhance community/law enforcement relationships. Think about each proposed plan.

1. How would you argue the merits of each proposal from a procedural justice perspective?
2. Would it make a difference if you knew that cameras were only 90 percent accurate and could be affected by weather conditions and

technical glitches? What level of accuracy would it take to guarantee "fair process"?

3. Would it make a difference to you if you knew that police look-out points were disproportionately represented in only certain neighborhoods of the city?

4. Would it make a difference if you knew that on any given day certain police officers arrest more than four times as many motorists for speeding and other types of violations than other police officers do?

5. Would it make a difference if you learned that the number of speeding tickets issued increased by tenfold when camera-based plans were put into effect?

6. Would the size of any fines rendered make any difference in how you thought about the fairness of each proposal? For instance, would you select the same plan to deal with fines of twenty dollars as you would to deal with fines of hundreds of dollars?

An Ethics Review Board: How to Structure It?

A second case examines fairness in a procedural process of determining ethics violations. Imagine the following.

> A small college in the United States is trying to set up a fair student ethics review board. The suggestion is made that the board should consist of six students selected by the faculty. If any student from the school was accused of an ethics violation, their case would be handled by this board. The accused student would first be interviewed by one of the board members and, if this board member thought there was sufficient evidence against the student, the case would be recommended for a full board discussion. The accused student could not be present at this board discussion, but they could represent their point of view in a written statement that would be read at the meeting by all board members. After a discussion of this, the board members would vote on what penalty, if any, to impose on the accused student. These penalties could range from expulsion from the school to some minimal financial fine. Records of all meetings would be kept

*strictly confidential and, because of this, there would be no chance to ap-
peal board decisions.*

1. How would you evaluate the fairness of this student ethical review
   system? What are its weaknesses and strong points in your mind?
2. How accepting do you think students accused of ethical violations
   would be of any penalties they might receive?
3. Would this be better or worse than having a single faculty member
   such as the Dean of Students or the President of the college rule on
   presented ethics violation cases?
4. How might you improve this type of peer review system?

Interactional Justice

Being Treated with Dignity

So far we have talked about process fairness in a rather formal sense. We
have looked at what particular procedural elements tend to be associated with perceptions that one was treated fairly. Much of the research
concerning these types of fairness issues examined justice perceptions in
fairly discrete disputes in which outcomes were either clearly favorable or
unfavorable to the contending disputants. For example, we might ask, did
I receive a fair trial outcome or a fair salary deal?

There is another way of looking at fair process that is a bit broader.
We can, for instance, ask larger questions such as does my husband or
wife generally treat me fairly, was this police officer fair in his or her
overall dealing with me, or is my teacher usually fair in her handling of
class assignments? In these types of fairness assessments, particular attention is paid to the overall quality of the exchange that occurred between
individuals, not just to whether particular procedural elements such
as opportunity for voice or decision-making consistency were present.
What is interesting is that sometimes we can perceive that fair process
rules are in place in a formal sense, but still feel that something is missing. What this missing thing is can be a bit hard to define, but it seems
to be related to the illusive concepts of respect and dignity. That is, I do
not want you to simply follow certain procedural rules and guidelines

in your interactions with me. I sometimes, additionally, want you to acknowledge me in a way that allows me to maintain my basic dignity and sense of worth. This turns out to be hugely important to us (Mikula, Petri and Tanzer 1990).

Of course, this brings up the very difficult question of what is dignity. It is easy to say what it is not. Dignity is not mocking or belittling or not taking another seriously. It is not being cruel or impolite. Dignity is also not conveyed by ignoring another person or dismissing their ideas in some rude manner. But what is it? People have different definitions of dignity, but most agree that at its core dignity involves a certain acknowledgement of another's humanity and a validation of their worth. It is also conveyed by a willingness to tell others the truth, to treat them with propriety, and to justify one's decisions to them. When these qualities are present, we will be more likely to say that we were treated fairly than when these qualities are not present (Bies and Moag 1986). This kind of fairness is an example of what some have called interactional justice (Tyler and Bies 1990; Bies 2001). Although it may be of great significance to us, it is harder to measure than the more objective procedural aspects of fair process.

To think about this a bit more, we might consider an example of a ball player who feels that she has been treated unfairly by a referee in a game, even though she is not be able to criticize the referee's actual calls or his adherence to formal game rules. Perhaps the referee turned away as she was talking to him, interrupted her explanation of events or seemed to dismiss her or mock her ideas in some other way. Even though the referee technically acted without fault, all of these small indignities might powerfully affect the ball player's interpretation of events, and her sense that she received fair game calls. These types of dignity effects can be compelling and have been demonstrated in a variety of contexts. For example, in a training program for police, newly recruited officers were taught how to implement procedures not just in an objectively fair manner, but also in a way that conveyed a sense of respect to others. These efforts increased both goodwill toward the police, and also acceptance and compliance with officer requests (Skogan, Van Craen and Hennessey 2015). These are not trivial findings.

Informational Justice

As we have seen, how we are treated by others matters greatly to us. We like to think our lives are significant and meaningful in the larger scheme of things. We also like to have sufficient advance notice about when important decisions about us will be made, and we are more satisfied with those decisions when we have been provided with information about why they were made. This is sometimes referred to as "informational justice," and it can be distinguished from the more interpersonal quality of interactional justice discussed above (Colquitt, Conlon, Wesson, Porter and Ng 2001; Kanfer, Sawyer, Earley and Lind 1987). What is especially interesting is that these informational justice effects are not dependent on receiving outcomes that are personally favorable to us. That is, even if we end up not getting what we want, we still find the process fairer if we are told the timing and the reasoning behind the decision-maker's choices.

Case Studies for Further Inquiry: What Is Dignity?

Is My Boss Behaving Fairly with Me?

To ponder the meaning of dignity a bit more, consider the following cases. The first case concerns ideas about dignity and fairness in a common employee-employer work situation. Imagine the following.

An employee named Mr. J. P. Littleton works in a big insurance company somewhere in the United States. Mr. Littleton serves in the position of managerial assistant for one of the company executives. In this job he is supposed to be at the disposal of the executive at all times, and to do whatever is necessary to enhance the company business. Mr. Littleton is called by his nickname Jimmy by his employer even though no one else in the company is addressed so familiarly. He is told what to do without being given an opportunity for input or comments on his part. Often his employer behaves as if Mr. Littleton is not in the room, even though he may be standing quite close to his boss. For instance, his employer will often talk to others in front of Mr. Littleton about his own personal health matters and sexual exploits. His boss additionally sometimes mocks and criticizes other employees in Mr. Littleton's presence, and refuses to take seriously Mr. Littleton's assertions about how uncomfortable this makes Mr. Littleton feel.

1. Is the above an example of unfair treatment or simply rude behavior? What is the difference?
2. How do power considerations figure into this? Would Mr. Littleton's treatment be more or less egregious if Mr. Littleton and his boss were equal peers in terms of company status and/or if Mr. Littleton actually held a higher position than his boss?
3. Are every situations of impoliteness also instances of unfair treatment? How do you differentiate these types of situations?

Is This Marriage Unfair?

Now in order to think more about the meaning of process fairness and dignity, consider the following:

A man named Sean and his wife Suzanne have been married for 15 years. Suzanne says that her husband treats her unfairly, although her husband vehemently denies this. Suzanne's chief complaint seems to be that her husband does not listen to her and ignores her opinions on all matters that come up between them. Suzanne also says that Sean sometimes humiliates her in front of others by mocking her ideas. He sometimes simply leaves the room when she is talking to him and does not answer her when she asks him questions.

1. Suzanne defines all of the above behavior as being "unfair." Is she right? What differentiates unfairness from simple mean spiritedness or boorishness?
2. Is there a certain element in Sean's treatment of Suzanne that you think is particularly unfair? What element?
3. Is the definition of unfair treatment in an intimate relationship such as marriage the same thing as unfairness in interactions between strangers? How might these differ?
4. What other questions might you want answered before you could definitely decide is Sean's treatment of Suzanne is "totally unfair" as Suzanne might say?

Why Does All of This Matter to Us?

A big question is why we care about procedural justice so much. Why are we not just concerned with what we receive or do not receive, and leave all of these process considerations aside? Researchers have pondered this question in different ways. Some posited that concern with procedural fairness often was just a proxy for an actual interest in distributive justice (Thibaut and Walker 1975). If we cannot control decision outcomes, controlling the decision-making process and having "voice" may be our next best thing. This is because we may think that we have a better chance of receiving personally favorable outcomes if we can represent our side of the story in any decision-making proceedings.

Some support can be found for these self-interest explanations of our concern for process. For instance, perhaps I received a traffic ticket and I am trying to argue before a traffic court judge that it was unfairly given to me. In such a case, I might value having a chance to represent my side of the story because I think that this will be more likely to lead to my traffic ticket being rescinded. Here my preference for voice would be simply instrumental. What is curious, however, is that research also shows that people often care about having the opportunity to express their opinions even when they know they have no chance of actually influencing the decision maker (Lind, Kanfer and Earley 1990; Tyler 2002). What does this mean? What might "voice" represent to individuals if it has no particular instrumental value? Beyond voice, why do we so strongly value being treated with dignity and respect?

These questions go back to our discussion of the human need to be validated and respected by others. In a just world, we believe we would receive affirmation that we "count." When we are allowed to have our say and are treated with dignity, this conveys an important message to us that we belong and that we are deserving enough to be taken seriously. Thus, how and if we are paid attention to affects our willingness to identify with our group (Tyler and Blader 2000), and gives us key feedback about our individual status and worth in the world (Miller 2001). The effects of being treated fairly appear to go beyond a simple affirmation of individual identity and, also, positively impact our broader social sense of self (Cooper and Scandura 2015; De Cremer and Tyler 2005).

As an example of this, we might imagine a situation in which a person is newly hired at a certain company. Perhaps this recently hired individual is at her first meeting with the other company employees. If these other employees treat this newly hired person with respect, if they politely ask her to express her opinions, if they listen to her ideas, her sense of herself may subtly shift. Being treated in this respectful manner may make her feel as if she has been accepted as a peer in this new, larger group. She is now part of a team and her self-image expands. She believes, to put it another way, that she matters.

Applications: Putting This Together to Debate Some Bigger Policy Issues

We have reviewed the major research theories of procedural justice and thought about the complexities involved when trying to determine if we have been treated fairly in a situation. As in the previous chapter, you will now be given the opportunity to use these ideas to critically analyze some important procedural justice policy issues. There are many such issues in our society. For example, how should we deal fairly with suspected terrorists and yet not jeopardize the security and safety of our citizens? How do we balance the right of an individual accused of a crime to face their accuser when the accuser is a child and might be traumatized by legal proceedings? Is it fair to not publish the name of a rape victim in the media if the name of the individual accused of the rape has been widely circulated to the public? These are complex issues and they have no easy answers.

In the following section, ideas and proposals pertaining to each of these issues will be presented and after each proposal a series of questions will be asked. There are no right or wrong answers to these questions. Rather, questions are included to help you think more deeply about these thorny policy problems, and to prod you to view arguments pertaining to them from a range of different perspectives.

Major Procedural Justice Dilemma #1: Dealing with Suspected Terrorists

There has been considerable discussion in the United States about how we should deal with individuals suspected of engaging in terrorist activities.

What does it mean to be "fair" with terrorists? Is this even a relevant question? Is it important to interact with all individuals with a certain modicum of respect? Is it important to interact even with suspected terrorists in a manner that allows them to maintain some basic level of dignity?

These are not trivial questions. Rather, they go to the heart of what it means to be committed to certain civilized standards of behavior and notions of fair process, and yet to balance this with practices that maintain reasonable levels of safety and security in society.

Proponents of treating everyone, even suspected terrorists, according to strict, fair treatment protocols would argue that if we violate these types of standards of decency, even in some extreme cases, then we begin to undermine what we stand for as a country. According to this view, everyone, no matter how potentially despicable or what level of risk they may pose to society, deserves to be treated in a manner that leaves their basic dignity intact.

Those on the con side of this argument might suggest that this thinking is naive. They would assert that some individuals, because of the brutal nature of the acts for which they are accused, have lost their right to any level of civility and respect from others. People who argue this position might also remind us that we should never sacrifice the potential security of many for the so-called fair-treatment of a few.

Construct arguments in support of both sides of this issue. What position seems most fair to you in an ideal world? Why?

Other points to ponder in terms of fairness:

1. Would the degree of certainty that you have that the terrorist suspect did, indeed, commit an act of terrorism affect how you think about this?
2. Should the fact that this person is simply accused but not convicted of a terrorist act make any difference in your considerations of how to treat him or her?
3. Should the awfulness or the degree of depravity of the crime for which they have been accused be taken into account? For example, should the individuals who were suspected of being involved in the bombing of the World Trade Center be treated in a similar manner as a person arrested for a much lesser crime?

4. Should the potential risk to the safety of U.S. citizens ever be considered when decisions are made about how to treat a suspected terrorist? For instance, if we thought that the suspected terrorist knows of a plan to destroy several major cities in the United States, should considerations of fair treatment be thrown out the window?

5. Would it make any difference if you knew *why* the suspected terrorist had committed his or her terrorist act? For instance, what if you knew that the alleged terrorist's parents had previously been killed in a drone strike by the United States? Would this change your thinking in any way?

6. Should the social and demographic conditions of the suspected terrorist be taken into account in any way? What if you knew that the alleged terrorist came from an extremely impoverished background, and he or she had been literally starving to death in the time period before their suspected terrorist activity? Is this relevant to any current treatment considerations?

7. Is it more or less fair to treat someone with dignity and respect if we know that they have severe emotional and mental problems and do not have a lot of control over their thoughts or behavior?

Major Procedural Justice Dilemma #2: Children Testifying in Court

Another important question is whether children should be required to testify in person in court proceedings when they accuse others of a crime such as physical or sexual abuse. This question has been a debated subject for some time. Those who would say "Yes, children should be required to testify" would point to the 6th amendment of the U.S. Constitution that guarantees defendants the right to face their accusers directly, and to be made aware of the nature of the accusations that are made against them.

Some are concerned, however, that if we are too zealous about protecting the rights of the accused that we put children at potential risk. For a child to publicly and directly face an adult defendant in court who they think has hurt or damaged them in some ways may be deeply traumatizing. The child may be afraid that the adult, who is much more powerful than they are, will harm them later if they testify publicly against them. Testifying may also force a child to relive the trauma of the original crime experience. If they are accusing a relative or someone who has been their caretaker of a crime, they may additionally worry about later abandonment and loss of love and protection from this person. The mere act of testifying in a formal and unfamiliar court setting may be incredibly intimidating and scary to many children.

The question, then, becomes how do we balance the needs of the child with the rights of the accused? This has been handled by different courts in different ways. In some jurisdictions, certain exceptions have been made concerning children's need to be physically present in court to testify. For example, sometimes videotaped interviews with the child can be used in lieu of direct testimony. In other cases, screens may be put in place in the courtroom to protect the child from having to look at the accused. Some people applaud these types of accommodations because they are felt to protect children from harm. Others, however, argue that they violate the constitutional rights of the accused to directly confront their accuser and should not be used.

Construct arguments in support of both sides of this issue. What position seems most fair to you in an ideal world? Why?

Other points to ponder in terms of fairness:

1. Would it make a difference in your thinking if the child involved was very young? In some cases, children as young as 3 or 4 years of age have been required to testify without accommodation in court. Is that "fair"?

2. What if the crime the child is accusing another of had a deeply traumatizing impact on the child. Should this be considered?

3. Should it matter if the accused is a relative of the child such as a parent or a sibling? Should different procedures be used in such cases?

4. How should the child's emotional state be factored into this, if at all? That is, should it make a difference if the child had a history of emotional and mental instability? Should such a child be forced to physically testify in court proceedings without accommodations?

5. How should the concerns of the accused be considered? For instance, what if the accused would not be able to see the demeanor of the child during his or her testimony. Would this be a serious violation of rights?

Major Allocation Dilemma #3: Dealing with Victims of Alleged Rape

A major issue in working with cases of alleged rape is whether or not to reveal the name of the victim to the public. People have varied opinions about this. An argument against doing this is that if victims' identities are revealed that this would discourage individuals, in general, from reporting rape. Some fear additionally that publicizing victims' names would violate the victims' rights to privacy and could unfairly stigmatize them.

Another view is that it is unfair not to disclose the victim's name if the name of the accused is made public. Certainly, publicizing the name of the accused, even if he or she is later found to be not guilty, would have the potential to permanently damage his or her reputation and standing in the community. Thus, some would argue that for the sake of even-handedness and consistency, the names of both the victim and the accused should either be withheld from the media or both made public.

Construct arguments in support of both sides of this issue. What positions seems most fair to you in an ideal world? Why?

Other points to ponder in terms of fairness:

1. Would it make a difference if you knew that the victim had a history of mental and emotional instability?
2. Should the fact that the accused is a very powerful and prominent person with an ability to impose great harm on others be considered in a decision about whether or not to release the victim's name?
3. Is it ever fair to take the past history of the victim into account when making a decision about whether or not to release his or her name in a case of alleged rape? For instance, what if the victim had been known in the past to have filed many unproved charges of rape against others? Would this fact be relevant at all to the present decision?
4. Would it be fairer to simply wait until after the trial verdict has been reached to release to the media both the names of the victim and the accused? Why or why not?

Summary

In this chapter a review of the major research findings in the area of procedural justice was presented. Procedural justice refers to the fairness of the processes of decision making. Several key themes emerge as we examine the literature in this area. First, perceptions of fair process exert a powerful impact on behavior and emotional reactions to events. When we think we have been treated fairly, we are more likely to comply with and accept others' decisions about us. Procedural justice often interacts with distributive justice, and it can soften the blow of receiving outcomes that are personally disadvantageous.

One important element individuals use to define fair procedures is the ability to have "voice" or input in decision making. When we are allowed to have such voice, we are more likely to believe that procedures are fair, even if we do not receive our preferred outcomes.

Procedural justice has also been examined in terms of the presence or absence of certain practices such as consistency in decision making, neutrality or lack of bias, accuracy, ability to remedy or correctability, ethicality or normative adherence, and representativeness or participation opportunities for all involved stakeholders. Perceptions of treatment fairness increase when these practices are in place.

Researchers in what is called interactional justice look at procedural fairness more broadly in terms of the overall quality of interactions between individuals. Certain interactional elements such as being treated with dignity and in a manner that conveys respect and a sense of belongingness positively impact justice judgments. Having others justify and give us sufficient advance notice about decisions that affect us, or having "informational justice," also adds to our sense of fair treatment.

Although there is considerable consensus among researchers that procedural justice greatly matters to us, there is some debate about why this is the case. One view posits that we care about having a fair process because we think that by having it we will have a better chance of receiving personally favorable outcomes. This instrumental view is contrasted with more relational models that emphasize the importance of fair treatment to our self-identity, conceptions of worth and sense of social acceptance from others. For further anlayses of the various nuances of procedural justice that have been researched, see Vermut and Steensma (2016).

References

Bies, Robert, J. 1986. "Beyond "Voice": The Influence of Decision-maker Justification and Sincerity on Procedural Justice Judgments." *Representative Research in Social Psychology.* 17(1): 3–14.

Bies, Robert J. and Joseph Moag. 1986. "Interactional Justice: Communication Criteria of Fairness." In *Research on Negotiaton in Organizations,* edited by Roy J. Lewicki, Blair H. Sheppard and Max H. Bazerman, 43–55, Greenwich, CT: JAI Press.

Bies, Robert J. 2001. "Interactional (In)justice: The Sacred and the Profane." In *Advances in Organizational Justice,* edited by Jerald Greenberg and Robert Cropanzano, 89–118. Palo Alto, CA: Stanford University Press.

Choi, Jaepil. 2003. "Outcome Favorability, Procedures and Individualism-Collectivism in Procedural Justice Perceptions." *Seoul Journal of Business.* 9 (1): 1–26.

Colquitt, Jason, Donald E. Conlon, Michael J. Wesson, Christopher Porter and K. Yee Ng. 2001. "Justice at the Millennium: A Meta-Analytic Review of 25 Years of Organizational Justice Research." *Journal of Applied Psychology.* 86 (3): 425–445.

Cooper, Cecily D. and Terri Scandura. 2015. "Getting to "Fair": Justice Interactions as Identity Negotiation." *Journal of Leadership and Organizational Studies.* 22 (4): 418–432.

Cropanzano, Russell and Jerald Greenberg. 1997. "Progress in Organizational Justice: Tunneling Through the Maze." In *International Review of Industrial and Organizational Psychology,* edited by Cary L. Cooper and Ivan T. Robertson, 317–372. New York, NY: Wiley.

De Cremer, David and Tom Tyler. 2005. "Managing Group Behaviour: The Interplay between Fairness, Self and Cooperation." In *Advances in Experimental Social Psychology,* edited by Mark P. Zanna, 151–218, New York, NY: Academic Press.

Deutsch, Morton. 1982. "Interdependence and Psychological Orientation." In *Cooperation and Helping Behavior,* edited by Valerian J. Delilega and Janusz Grzelak, 247–270. New York, NY: Academic Press.

Folger, Robert, David D. Rosenfield, Janet Grove and Louise L. Corkran. 1979. "Effects of "Voice" and Peer Opinions and Responses to Inequity." *Journal of Personality and Social Psychology.* 37 (12): 2253–2261.

Kanfer, Ruth, John Sawyer, Chirstopher Earley and Edgar Allen Lind. 1987. "Fairness and Participation in Evaluation Procedures: Effects on Task Attitudes and Performance." *Social Justice Research.* 1:235–249.

Leventhal, Gerald. 1980. "What Should be Done with Equity Theory? New Approaches to the Study of Fairness in Social Relationships." In *Social Exchange,* edited by Kenneth J. Gergen, Martin S. Greenberg and Richard H. Willis, 27–55. New York, NY: Plenum.

Lind, Edgar Allen, Ruth Kanfer and P. Christopher Earley. 1990. "Voice, Control and Procedural Justice: Instrumental and Noninstrumental Concerns in Fairness Judgments." *Journal of Personality and Social Psychology.* 59 (5): 952–959.

Lind, Edgar Allen and Tom R. Tyler. 1988. *The Social Psychology of Procedural Justice.* New York, NY: Plenum.

Mikula, Gerald, Birgit Petri and Norbert K. Tanzer. 1990. "What People Regard as Unjust: Types and Structures of Everyday Experiences of Injustice." *European Journal of Social Psychology.* 20 (2): 133–149.

Miller, Dale T. 2001. "Disrespect and the Experience of Injustice." *Annual Review of Psychology.* 52: 527–553.

Potter, Paula W. 2006. "Procedural Justice, Voice Effects and Sham: Examining the Decision- Maker from a Research Context." *Journal of Organizational Culture, Communications and Conflict.* 10 (2): 61–75.

Rusbult, Caryl and Paul P. Van Lange. 1996. "Interdependence Processes." In *Social Psychology,* edited by Edward T. Higgins and Arie W. Kruglanski, 564–596. New York, NY: Guilford Press.

Skogan, Wesley G., Maarten Van Craen and Cari Hennessey. 2015. "Training Police for Procedural Justice." *Journal of Experimental Criminality.* 11 (3): 319–334.

Thibaut, John and Laurens L. Walker. 1975. *Procedural Justice: A Psychological Analysis.* Hillsdale, NJ: Lawrence Erlbaum Associates.

Tyler, Tom R. 1988. "What is Procedural Justice? Criteria used by Citizens to Assess the Fairness of Legal Procedures." *Law and Society Review.* 22 (1): 103–135.

Tyler, Tom R. 2002. "Social Justice: Outcome and Procedure." *International Journal of Psychology.* 35 (2): 117–125.

Tyler, Tom R. and Robert J. Bies. 1990. " Interpersonal Aspects of Procedural Justice." In *Applied Psychology in Business Settings,* edited by John S. Carroll, 77–98. Hillsdale, NJ: Lawrence Erlbaum Associates.

Tyler, Tom R. and Steven L. Blader. 2000. *Cooperation in Groups: Procedural Justice, Social Identity and Behavioral Engagement.* Philadelphia, PA: Psychology Press.

Van den Bos, Kees and Edgar Allen Lind, 2002. "Uncertainty Management by Means of Fairness Judgments." In *Advances in Experimental Social Psychology,* edited by Mark P. Zanna, 1–60. New York, NY: Academic Press.

Van Prooijen, Jan Willem, Kees Van den Bos and Hank A.M. Wilke. 2004. "Group Belongingness and Procedural Justice: Social Inclusion and Exclusion by Peers Affects the Psychology of Voice." *Journal of Personality and Social Psychology.* 87: 66–79.

Van Prooijen, Jan Willem. 2009. "Procedural Justice as Autonomy Regulation." *Journal of Personality and Social Psychology.* 96: 1166–1180.

Vermut, Riël and Herman Steensma. 2016. "Procedural Justice." In *The Handbook of Social Justice Theory and Research,* edited by Clara Sabbagh and Manfred Schmitt, 219–236, New York, NY: Springer.

CHAPTER 3

Retributive Justice

Abstract

In this chapter a review of the major research findings in the area of retributive justice is presented. Retributive justice concerns the fairness of the allocation of punishment for individuals who violate the law. It examines questions such as who in a just society should be punished, for what reason, and in what manner. Major chapter headings include the purpose of punishment, who should we punish, and how should we punish. Each of these major sections is further divided into several subsections.

Multiple topics are explored within each of these various chapter sections. For instance, the goals of different types of punishment systems are analyzed, and the use of "not guilty by reason of insanity" and "guilty but mentally ill" verdicts are discussed. Differences between how the law and how psychology understand the notion of guilt are also examined. Particular attention is paid to a consideration of the use of the death penalty in the United States because it is the most dramatic and the most controversial form of punishment that we have available to us.

Definition of Retributive Justice

In Chapters 1 and 2 we discussed distributive and procedural justice. We have seen the powerful impact both these types of justice can have on how we respond to events in our world, and we have talked about why each is so important to us. Now we are going to shift our perspective again. In this chapter we will look at what is called retributive justice. Retributive justice concerns the fairness of the allocation of punishment in society. Many situations involve decisions about the use of punishment. For instance, different types of punishment can be used by parents to discipline their children, by teachers to keep their classrooms places of learning, by employers to reprimand employees who violate workplace rules, and even by individuals in interpersonal relationships to correct partners for various kinds of perceived mistreatment. However, since most research on the concept of retributive justice has been in the legal arena, that is what we will concentrate on in this chapter, although some examples from other areas will be given, as well.

When we talk of retributive justice, we must deal with basic questions such as who should be punished, why, how, and for what. These are extremely important questions to raise, and they go to the heart of our conception of a well-ordered society.

To start thinking about this we might imagine a society called Society Y in which no formal systems of punishments exist. Here there are no laws, no prisons, no fines, no courts, and no judges because none is needed. Everyone in Society Y seems to get along very well most of the time; and when minor disputes among individuals arise, the people involved handle them directly and informally with minimal public conflict.

Consider what images come to your mind when you reflect on this type of hypothetical society. Would Society Y be a good place to live? Can you even imagine it? Would this society probably be a kind of utopia, or would it more likely be a place where people would have to be coerced in some manner to remain so apparently conflict free?

How we answer these questions reveals some of our implicit assumptions about human nature. Are people naturally good? If left to their own devices, and if sufficient resources are provided, would people be apt to cooperate with one another and flourish? Or would society, no matter how rich, be likely to evolve into a kind of anarchy without some sort of structures in place to negatively sanction those who commit harm to others? As we ponder these issues, we can begin to reflect on the function and purpose of our legal punishment systems. Who and why should we punish? How wide should our punishment net be? For what should we punish? What does it mean to over punish someone or punish him or her too harshly? What does it mean to have "just" systems of punishment? What type of society are we trying to create when we punish others? These are the types of topics we will be dealing with in this chapter.

The Purpose of Punishment

We will start our discussion by examining the purpose of punishment. As we shall see, we can have very different types of goals in mind when we decide to punish others. Implementation strategies to meet these different types of goals will also have differential impacts both on the individual who is punished and on the society at large (Vidmar and Miller 1980).

Just Stop Doing That

The simplest and most straightforward purpose of punishment is to try to get the perpetrator to just stop doing the inappropriate or unwanted behavior (Palmetti and Russo 2011). Imagine a young child who is playing a game of cards with her brother. The brother and his sister begin to argue, and then the sister goes over to her brother and starts repeatedly pinching him on his arm. At this point, the children's mother comes in the room and screams at her daughter saying in a loud voice, "Stop that right now or else. . ." The little girl looks up startled, and stops pinching her bother. Thus, the mother's goal in controlling her child's behavior is achieved. Even though she did not use direct punishment, her indirect threat of punishment was enough to stop her daughter's inappropriate pinching.

This example shows a very instrumental, utilitarian use of punishment. The punishment's purpose is to have the violator (in this case the little girl) simply cease doing what she is doing. While we know that the mother's behavior was effective in the short-term, we would be less certain about the longer-term impact of her behavior on her child. For example, would the child start pinching her brother again when the mother left the room? Would she become more prone to violence in the future? This would depend on many factors such as the child's relationship with her mother and their previous history together; but, in general, we know that the type of punishment that the mother used tends to be better at causing temporary suppression rather than longer-term elimination of targeted negative behaviors (Palmetti and Russo 2011).

Although the above example does not concern the use of punishment in a legal sense, the behavioral principles involved in legal and non-legal situations would be similar: An unwanted behavior occurs that someone in authority wants stopped. For instance, a law enforcement officer might sternly tell party goers who are in violation of certain community noise ordinances to shut down their music or face receiving a citation. A motorist who is speeding might be pulled over by a policeman, issued a warning ticket "just this one time," and told to slow down. In all of these cases, the goal of the authorities is to use the implied threat of later punishment to get the violator to alter their current actions.

That Is Not Worth It

Sometimes we can use the simple threat of punishment to prevent violations from ever occurring in the first place (Gibbs 1968; Nagin 1998). For example, perhaps the mother of the little girl who is prone to bad behavior could have told the little girl that she would be grounded for a week if she ever even considered doing anything as nasty as pinching her brother. Or, perhaps if we know that we would be put in jail for a first arrest of drunk driving, we might be more apt to resist ever drinking and driving than if we thought that if we were caught drunk we would only be given a minor financial fine. These examples illustrate the "get tough on crime" philosophy. The belief is that if the costs of committing a crime can be made high enough, this should deter potential offenders of the law from acting (Cullen, Clark and Wozniak 1985). We may, for instance, not rob the store if we know that if we were caught we would be publicly hanged.

Of course, this get-tough philosophy assumes that people decide to commit most crimes on the basis of very rational considerations. We know, in fact, that many criminals are driven as much by impulse and emotion as they are by logical cost–benefit analyses. We also know that people are not very good at calculating real risks and at assessing probabilities of getting caught if they do take risks (Tversky and Kahneman 1974). All of this complicates our ability to predict deterrence effects on the basis of the severity of potential punishment alone.

Reform or Change the Offender

There are other goals we can have when we punish people. For instance, we may not simply want to stop or prevent the offender from engaging in some act out of fear or worry about getting caught; rather, we may want to reform him or her in some more basic way (Kaufman 1960). This emphasis on rehabilitation and reduction of future recidivism is sometimes called a constructionist approach to criminal justice (Fondacaro, Koppel, O'Toole and Crain 2015; Wenzel, Okimoto, Feather and Platow 2008). To think about this a bit more, we can go back to our example of a mother reprimanding her daughter for pinching her brother. Let's think of a slightly changed version of this episode. This time, after the mother screamed at her daughter, she also began to explain to her daughter why her behavior had been wrong. She talked about how badly being pinched on the arm made her brother feel and how disappointed she was in her daughter's actions. She talked about what she expected from her daughter, and she explained why we cannot have people just go around pinching others when they are upset. Perhaps, after the mother finished saying all of this, her daughter would feel a change of heart. Maybe she would stop pinching her brother not only because she was afraid of what her mother would do to her if she pinched him again, but also because now she felt differently about the whole act of pinching. If this occurred we might say that the daughter was "reformed." She is no longer quite what she was before, and now would probably need fewer threats from her mother to stop her from pinching others in the future.

The above represents the reform goal of punishment. Through a punishment system, we try to get the offender to learn to shift their perspective about their past criminal actions and begin to see themselves and their situation differently. We want the offender to be remorseful and to mean it when and if they say they are sorry for what they have done. Having this type of change in attitude should decrease the probability that the offender will engage in a similar kind of crime again, even when external controls on his or her behavior are not present. We, as victims, may also feel better if we think that the offender truly understands that what he or she did to us was wrong (Funk, McGeer and Gollwitzer 2014).

How we implement this type of attitude shift and its necessity for structuring "effective" punishment, of course, can be debated. What if reform efforts are not successful? We might imagine someone who was sentenced to 5 years in prison for committing a robbery and has now served those 5 years. Would we be morally justified in requiring that this person also change his or her attitude before getting out of prison, even though he or she spent the required time in confinement? How, in fact, would we assess such an attitude change? Would we use a test? Would we need some type of lie-detection procedure to go with this? These are difficult questions. Clearly, even if we think that the goal of reform in punishment systems is commendable, its fair implementation can be problematic.

Making It up to the Victim

So far we have just been talking of ways to deal with an individual who has violated some rules or laws. However, we can also ask, "What of the victim?" Should considerations of the victim's feelings and needs influence how we deal with the offender? To think about this a bit more, we can go back to our brother-and-sister-at-play example. This time, though, we can imagine that the mother, after witnessing her daughter pinching her brother on the arm, dealt with the punishment situation slightly differently. In this scenario, instead of simply telling her daughter to stop what she was doing "or else. . .," she additionally told her daughter that she would have to make it up to her brother in some way. That is, she would have to acknowledge to her brother that what she did was wrong and to provide him with some kind of mutually agreed-upon restitution. Perhaps the little girl could agree to do her brother's chores for a day, or could offer to buy him a special toy that he wanted. Whatever it was, these efforts would be carried out by the little girl not just to convey that she was sorry for what she did, but also to bring a kind of balance back to the situation. She pinched her brother and this was bad; but by enacting these "make-up behaviors", a kind of good will between them could be restored.

This form of retributive justice, sometimes called "restorative justice," is focused more on the victim's needs and rights (Braithwaite 2007; Cohen 2016). It can be used in a variety of ways. For instance, we might imagine that someone trashed our lawn one night as a Halloween prank. From a restorative justice point of view those who were later found to be guilty of this act should not just have to pay a fine or be given some other type of penalty. Rather, they should also have to do something that has a direct impact on the damage they created. For instance, perhaps an agreement could be made that those who damaged the lawn would have to do free lawn work for the homeowner for a month or two. Or perhaps they could plant trees in the neighborhood or pick up trash on the community clean-up day. The specifics of their "punishment" would not matter as much as a sense that by doing it some type of wholeness or order was restored to that which had been violated. The victim is given back a sense of dignity and the offenders have been reinstated in society.

These types of punishment systems are based on a premise that something can be restored after a crime of some type has been committed. There may be times when the offense may have been so vile or horrific that bringing balance back is not possible. We can think of instances such as when a gruesome rape or murder is committed in which the damage and pain caused to the victim appear irreparable. In these cases attempts to create a sense of restorative justice might be more difficult to achieve. However, it may not always be restoration, per se, that victims seek. Rather, at times what a victim or victim's family may want is simple acknowledgment of the depth of the pain they were made to suffer (Strang 2002; Digman 2005; Cohen 2016). This is similar to our discussion of the importance of having voice in legal proceedings in the last chapter on procedural justice. What we may want as victims is a recognition that we count and that our feelings and pain matter. We may also want an admission from the offender that our hurt was undeserved. This kind of acknowledgment would not make up in any way for the pain the victim suffered, but could represent a beginning step in the process of reestablishing victim dignity.

Getting Even

The above discussion of restorative justice focused on restoration in a rather positive sense. Something is built or made better to make up for some created wrong. We can, however, imagine a different type of restoration in which balance is sought in a more negative way. This might be referred to as "just deserts" or "an eye for an eye" justice (French 2001;

Darley and Pittman 2003). For instance, if you steal a loaf of bread I cut off your hand. If you cause me great pain I cause you similar pain through torture or deprivation of some type. Thus, I match what you have done to me by making you experience a similar hurt. We may have different ideas about whether this type of attempted balancing is good or just, but it is not unheard of in our current criminal justice system. For example, we might consider the use of the death penalty for horrendous crimes of murder to be an example of this type of justice motive. You have taken a life so we must make you pay by taking yours, as well. We will talk more about the death penalty later in this chapter, but suffice it to say here that this type of "an eye for an eye" justice can have negative side effects and may increase rather than decrease the level of violence and aggression in society.

Reestablishing Order in Society

The previous discussion dealt with consideration of punishment's impact on the individual offender or the crime victim. But what are the broader societal functions of punishment? Why do we punish individuals for the sake of society?

One broader goal of punishment is to reestablish order and stability to our social systems (Carlsmith, Darley and Robinson 2002). When someone breaks a law or commits a crime, a part of our social fabric is broken, as well. If we had no system of law enforcement we would have no way of sanctioning individuals who cause harm to others. In such a situation, if individuals wanted to seek restitution for some act committed against them, they would have to take matters into their own hands. For instance, if you hurt someone in my family, I might feel compelled to equally hurt someone in your family. This could then lead to further retaliation and a never-ending cycle of violence and vigilantism. One function of having a formal system of punishments is to prevent this sort of negative cycle from occurring. We may feel, that is, that we do not have to personally avenge every hurt that we experience because we have learned to believe and trust in our system of justice to do that for us. This belief is hugely important to maintaining an ordered and regulated society.

Sending a Symbolic Message to Society About What Is Important to Us

An even more basic social goal of punishment is to affirm our core values as a society (Carlsmith and Darley 2008; Wenzel, Okimoto, Feather and Platow 2008). To think about this we might return once again to our example of a brother and sister having an argument in which the sister pinches her brother on his arm. This time, however, we can imagine that the brother and sister were members of some club called "The Blue Jays," and that the incident took place during one of the weekly Blue Jay meetings. Perhaps the mother of these two children was a Blue Jay leader. In this case, when she told her daughter to stop pinching her brother, she might not have been solely directing her comments to her daughter alone. Rather, she might have been trying additionally to send a message to the larger group of Blue Jays that this behavior of her daughter's did not reflect Blue Jay values. It did not represent how real and true Blue Jays should act! Thus, in this process, the mother could both reprimand her daughter and at the same time attempt to strengthen the sense of unity and identity among all Blue Jay club members.

This value affirmation aspect of punishment can be quite powerful. For instance, when we punish rapists with harsh and tough sentences we might not only do this simply because we think rape is bad, but also do this because we want to send a clear message to the world that rapists do not represent who we are and what we stand for as a society.

Case Studies for Further Inquiry: What Is Appropriate Punishment?

A Sex Offender Gets His Day in Court

To think about these issues concerning the purpose of punishment a bit more, consider the following hypothetical cases. The first case concerns a man accused of a sexual offense against a child. Imagine the following:

> *A middle-aged man in a certain community is found guilty of raping a 5-year-old child. This man has had multiple past convictions for*

similar acts. The judge in this case must decide what a fair punishment for this man's crime should be. Imagine for the purpose of this exercise that the judge has two punishment options to choose from.

One option is to rule that this man must take certain drugs daily that take away his sexual desire and feelings of aggressiveness. The man would have to have his drug taking strictly monitored, and he would have to put up with negative side effects that the drugs sometimes cause such as dizziness and nausea. He would have to take these drugs for life. If he stayed with this regimen, he would be able to remain to live and work in the community.

Another option would be to make this man serve a specific number of years in prison for his crime. For example, he might be given a sentence of 25 years with no chance for parole. After he served his time, he would be rereleased into the community.

1. Would either of these punishment options be fair? What purpose would they serve? In what way might they be too little or too much?
2. Does the heinousness of the crime matter in your thinking about punishment appropriateness? What if this sex offender, for instance, not only raped children, but also brutally beat them during this act as well? Would that information be relevant to you?
3. Would the offender's past role in society matter? That is, should he be punished more or less or differently if he held an important role in society such as being a priest or a teacher? Why or why not?
4. Should the fact that the offender grew up in an environment in which he experienced abuse as a child himself be taken into account when you think about appropriate punishment for him now?

A Cheating Scandal: What Should Punishment Mean Here?

A second case examines punishment fairness and appropriateness in deliberations about student cheating. Imagine the following.

A student at a small liberal arts college was caught cheating on an exam. This is the student's first cheating offense. The student claimed that she cheated because she was feeling desperate. She said that she had been sick the night before the incident and unable to study for the exam on which she cheated. She worried that if she flunked the exam she would lose her financial scholarship to the school. She further stated that this was the only time in her life that she had ever cheated on an exam.

The authorities at the college are trying to decide what punishment to give this student. Suggested punishments include having the student simply pay a fine, having her write an essay about why cheating is wrong that would be published under her name in the school paper, or expelling her from the school for gross misconduct and violation of the school's ethical code.

1. Which of the suggested punishments seem most appropriate and fair to you and why? If none of them do, what would seem appropriate to you?
2. What function would each punishment serve?
3. Does the fact that this is a first offense for her alter your thinking in any way?
4. Does the fact that this student is a financial scholarship student or that she was ill the night before her exam affect how you think about her case?
5. Would the fact that you know this college to be a very old and prestigious institution influence how you think about what is the best thing to do here?

Whom Should We Punish?

In the previous section we talked about different reasons that we punish others, but we did not address how we should decide if a person is deserving of punishment in the first place. We can start thinking about this by pondering the question of what it means to be guilty of something. Clearly, if we had no notion of guilt we would understand the idea of punishment very differently. So we can ask this basic question. When I say you are guilty of something in a legal sense what does it mean? What am I saying about you?

Legal Guilt: Were You Just Insane?

The law is very complicated and nuanced in its treatment of the basic concept of guilt (Costanzo 2004; Greene and Heilbrun 2011). If a court finds that a person committed an illegal act, this does not necessarily mean that the court will find that person legally "guilty," and punish them accordingly. Rather, in a majority of states, we cannot be held legally guilty for something if, when we committed a crime, we were not aware of the implications of what we did. In such a case we can be declared to be legally insane and, therefore, "not guilty" of our crime. This is the essence of the general reasoning behind these types of "not guilty by reason of insanity" verdicts, although specific statutory language defining legal insanity varies from state to state. Three states do not allow these defenses to be used at all. In some states such as Texas, "not guilty by reason of insanity" is construed very narrowly to mean that the individual who committed the crime was not able, in any manner, to understand the consequences of their actions or to distinguish the wrongfulness of their behavior. And, in other states, more general statutory language is employed in which insanity is described as being a state in which one was unable to "fully appreciate" the implications of what one did, or a condition in which one exhibited a "substantially impaired" ability to conform one's conduct to the law. Basically, in all these jurisdictions in which some form of an insanity defense is allowed, what the courts are saying is that we cannot define a person to be guilty of some act if they are completely misguided about the effects of that act. If I stabbed you with my knife and killed you, for example, but I thought I was fighting Dracula and trying to remove the curse of the undead, can you say I am guilty of murder? According to some interpretations of the law in some states, the answer would be no.

A few more points can be made about this concept of legal insanity. First, legal insanity and psychiatric notions of insanity are very different (Slobogin, Hafemeister, Mossman and Reisner 2013). Legal insanity means that we were unaware of what we were doing *at the moment we committed the crime*. Thus, simply having a psychiatric diagnosis such as paranoid schizophrenia or bipolar disorder would not alleviate us from potential criminal guilt. Rather, we must prove that our state of mind was substantially impaired during the very narrow window of time during which the crime took place. This, it turns out, is often hard to do, and insanity as a legal defense is rarely used at all, and even less frequently used successfully. Specifically, it is used less than 1 percent of the time; and of those instances when it is used, it is successful only 25 percent of the time (Greene and Heilbrun 2011).

Another misconception about legal insanity is that if we are declared to be insane and therefore "not guilty" of some crime, we will get off completely free and pay no penalty for our actions. In actuality, many times those who violate the law and then are defined as being insane in a legal sense are placed in mental institutions for indeterminate periods. Here the time they serve in confinement might actually end up being more than it would have been if they had been sentenced to more traditional prisons (Greene and Heilbrun 2011). Interestingly, in some jurisdictions, an offender can be defined as being guilty and legally insane at the same time by use of a "Guilty but Mentally Ill" verdict (Poulson, Wuensch and Brondino 1998). In these cases, the goal of holding a person accountable for a crime and of referring individuals to appropriate psychiatric treatment for their condition are simultaneously upheld.

Did You Feel Guilty?

Not only is the concept of legal insanity different from the concept of psychiatric insanity (which is not often used anymore), but also the whole notion of guilt is understood differently in the fields of law and psychology (Eaves, Ogloff and Roesch 2000). In legal parlance to be guilty of something means that we violated some law in a manner for which we should be punished. If we jay walked across some street and that was against the town ordinances, we are guilty whether we think this is a good, bad or indifferent law, and whether we are sorry or not sorry for what we did. Psychological guilt, on the other hand, tends to be much more feeling oriented. For example, we might have felt feel badly when we yelled at our sister or experienced remorse when we fought with our friend. If so, in a psychological sense, we might say that we experienced a state of guilt.

I Did Not Mean to Do That!

We have been talking about how a person's ability to comprehend the consequences of what he or she did should be weighed in considerations of legal guilt. Another factor that the law uses to calculate the degree of wrongfulness of an act is the intentionality of the offender at the time he or she committed the crime (Adler, Mueller and Laufer 2009). To consider this, we can imagine different types of scenarios. In the first scenario, a motorist on a highway willfully smashes his car into another vehicle with the intention of harming the driver of that vehicle because he is angry about being cut off in traffic. The driver of the first vehicle is not injured, but the motorist whose car was smashed into dies. Contrast that with a second scenario in which, again, a motorist is killed after her car is hit by another driver. In this case, though, the driver did not purposefully hit the second car. Rather she simply lost control of her vehicle because she was driving too fast for conditions on a rainy night and, in that process, hit the second vehicle.

Should both of these violations of the law be treated the same way? After all, in both cases someone died because of the direct actions of another. The law would say "no" they should not be treated similarly, and that the punishment for the driver in the first scenario should be much greater than the punishment given to the driver in the second scenario because the motivation of the drivers was so different.

In the above example, the impact of the drivers' behavior was the same, but the specific actions that led to this impact were very different. Sometimes the reverse situation can be the case. That is, sometimes similar recklessness can lead to very different outcomes. This is also considered in assessments of legal blame (Adler, Mueller and Laufer 2009). For instance, imagine that a man parks his car on a hill, forgets to set his brake, and walks away. In the first case, when he comes back to find his car, he notices that it had just started to roll down a hill, but hit a bush and came to a stop. No one was hurt and the car is undamaged. In a second case, the man parks his car in the same manner and similarly forgets to set his brake. This time, however, there is no bush to stop the car when it starts to move down the hill. The car rolls completely down the hill and just when it gets to the bottom a young child jumps in front of it looking for her ball. The car hits her and she is killed. Here, although the behavior of the man who parked his car carelessly was exactly the same, the legal penalty he would have to pay in the second case would be much greater than in the first case.

I Cannot Think Through That

Another factor that may be taken into account when thinking about punishment appropriateness is the cognitive capacity of the offender in a more general sense. That is, does the offender have sufficient mental skills to be able to reason, at least minimally effectively, about the results of his or her actions? If the answer is "no," the law suggests that certain degrees of extreme punishment may not be fair. In a landmark Supreme Court decision (*Atkins v. Virginia* 2002), for example, the court ruled that individuals determined to have an IQ below a certain level could not receive the death penalty for any crime he or she committed, no matter how heinous. And, in another groundbreaking ruling (*Roper v. Simmons* 2005), the court asserted that children under the age of 18 could not be given the death penalty. This decision was based, in part, on the assessment that the brains of juveniles were not fully developed. Because of this, juveniles were considered to be more subject to impulse and distraction, and were thought to lack the reasoning ability of more mature adults. In both of these cases, individuals can be determined to "be guilty" of something, but not fully culpable enough to pay for their crimes with the ultimate penalty of death.

Case Studies for Further Inquiry: How Do I Determine That?

I Am Too Young to Be Punished So Severely

The first case focuses on the issue of age in an incident involving two young men convicted of murder. Imagine the following.

> *Two teenagers named Sam and Peter are convicted of the brutal murder of an older woman. The murder involved multiply stabbing and beating a completely helpless individual. Both boys were witnessed to have*

been laughing and mocking their victim when they killed her. Sam was 18 years old when he committed the crime and his friend Peter at the time was just one month shy of his 18th birthday. Sam is given the death penalty for his crime, whereas his friend Peter, because of his age, is given life imprisonment.

In the law, these types of dichotomous distinctions sometimes have to be made. One has to draw the line somewhere and, in this case, one boy is defined as being an adult and one is defined as being a juvenile.

1. Is this differentiation between Sam and Peter's punishment fair? Why or why not?
2. Would you think about this differently if Sam was 18 years old and Peter was 12 years old? What age (if any) should be used as a cutoff point when thinking about death penalty appropriateness?
3. Should the heinousness of the crime committed be taken into account when age factors are considered?

I Did Not Want to Hurt You

The second case focuses on how we determine intentionality in a criminal case. Imagine the following:

A woman and her husband are having a verbal argument. In the midst of this argument, the woman pushes her husband who is standing near the top of the stairs. He steps back, loses his balance, and falls down the stairs to his death. The wife claims that this was a complete accident. She said she pushed her husband because he was physically threatening her. She said that she pushed him to get him to back off. The investigating officers are not so sure that this is a truthful account. The problem, though, is that there were only two people at this incident, and one of them is now deceased.

This case reflects the difficulty of assessing intentionality when there are no witnesses to a potential criminal act.

1. What questions would you like to ask the wife if you were investigating this case?

2. How can we ever really know what is in someone's mind at the time of a "crime"?

3. Is it possible that someone who harmed another might really not know whether their actions were intentional or not? If so, what would be an example of that?

4. What if this husband simply stepped back after he was pushed, and then regained his balance and walked away? Would the wife be guilty of any crime at all in your eyes if this was all that occurred?

What Is Fair Punishment?

So far in this chapter we have discussed the purpose of punishment and factors that are taken into account in the assessment of legal guilt for some action. But up until now we have not discussed how we should punish others when they violate the law. What is fair punishment? What is excessive? What is too lenient punishment? These are all important questions. Obviously, when we punish others we have a wide range of punishment options from which to choose. We can, for instance, give someone a financial penalty, we can confine them to prison for a certain period of time, we can torture or harm them physically in some way, or we can even kill them.

In the following sections, we will be discussing mainly this last punishment option of death. We will do this both because the death penalty is the most contentious form of punishment that we have, and because its use brings up so many significant moral and legal issues.

The death penalty is theoretically used when we define some crime to be so heinous and so outside the norms of civilized behavior that we, as a society, decide that the person who committed this type of crime should not be allowed to live anymore. When we seek death for a violator of the law we are implicitly saying that there can be no act of restorative justice, besides death, to make up for what he or she has done. We use this penalty when we think the offender does not deserve a second chance or a try at some type of rehabilitation. By their horrendous act they have lost this right.

The above represents some of our stated goals for the weighty decision to sentence a person to death for a crime that they committed. But are these legitimate goals? Is the death penalty fairly used? Is it an effective deterrent of crime? Is its use moral? To begin to think about these questions, let's first review a brief history of the use of the death penalty in the United States.

The Death Penalty in the United States

Although early on in the United States some individuals were executed for the crime of rape, now the death penalty is usually reserved only for those who have been convicted of the crime of murder. In 1972 the Supreme Court (*Furman v. Georgia*) struck down the use of capital punishment at both the federal and state level, stating that its use violated the 8th amendment against cruel and unusual punishment, and the 14th amendment which guaranteed a right to equal protection under the law. Then in 1976 (*Gregg v. Georgia*) the Court ruled that the death penalty could be reinstated if a two part trial process was used in which, first, defendant guilt or innocence was determined and, then, a separate decision about sentencing was made in which both aggravating and mitigating factors were weighed. Since 1976 there have been 1,437 executions enacted in the United States. Currently, the death penalty can be used in 30 states. Not only are there differences across states in terms of whether the death penalty can or cannot be legally used, but there is also tremendous variability in the frequency of its use among states that do allow it (Death Penalty Information Center 2016).

Thus, there is a considerable lack of agreement about when, where, and if we should ever use this ultimate form of punishment. When we think about the death penalty, hard issues are raised. Let's examine a few of these.

Is the Death Penalty as Used Today in the United States "Cruel and Unusual"?

It can be argued that the death penalty is a type of state-sponsored murder and that its use is barbaric and undermining of core values that admonish us to respect all human life. The reasoning here is that if murder is wrong in the first place, why would a second murder in some way make up for that first wrong? Others suggest that, to the contrary, use of the death penalty reaffirms respect for life because it upholds the worth and value of the victim's life. According to this view, when we execute someone who has taken another's life we are honoring and paying a kind of homage to the life that was lost (Bedan 2005).

The way the death penalty is actually implemented has also been the subject of some controversy and debate. Many times, for instance, because of the length of appeal processes, individuals on death row may have to wait 15 years or more for their execution day. In addition, executions can be botched even when using the lethal injection protocols that are more commonly in place now in states, and deaths can be agonizingly slow and painful. The question is whether subjecting death row inmates to this possible agony is justified because of the great pain the offender caused the victims and their families to suffer, or is this a kind of state-inflicted torture that is outside the bounds of civilized behavior.

What If Mistakes Are Made?

The law, of course, is not perfect. Those in authority sometimes make mistakes and innocent people may be executed for crimes they did not commit. And, thanks to the use of new DNA evidence, we know that this is not just a theoretical argument anymore. Hundreds of people who were wrongfully convicted have now been exonerated on the basis of DNA evidence (The Innocence Project 2016). The question is what do we do with this knowledge? What error rate for executions should we tolerate as a society? For instance, should we say that something like a 5 percent wrongful execution rate is not bad if we can be accurate 95 percent of the time, or is even one wrongful death unsupportable? These, of course, are difficult questions that go to the heart of our idea about the purpose and value of human life.

Is the Death Penalty Consistently Used?

As we discussed previously, the use of the death penalty varies tremendously state by state, and people who commit similar crimes do not all receive the same penalty (Smith 2011). The punishment would be vastly different, for example, if someone committed the same murder in Alabama, where the death penalty is legal, versus in Massachusetts where the law does not allow the death penalty. Furthermore, even among states that do allow the death penalty, its rate of implementation is hugely different. Two states, Texas and Oklahoma, for instance, account for almost half of the 1,437 executions that have occurred since 1976, the year the death penalty was reinstated in the United States (Death Penalty Information Center 2016). Among all individuals who are convicted of murder, it should be noted, only a very small percentage are ever sentenced to death, and within that group an even smaller number are actually executed (Greene and Heilbrun 2011). The question is whether these statistics should comfort us because they show the great care we take when we use this sentence, or if they indicate the existence of a kind of unsettling arbitrariness in the system that ought to be troubling. The answer to this is often in the eyes of the beholder.

We do know that the race of those involved seems to make a difference in sentencing. If the victim is white, for example, there is a disproportionately higher chance that the offender will be given the death penalty than if the victim is not white. And those who are poor receive this sentence at a higher rate than those who have lots of money (Death Penalty Information Center 2016).

Does Use of the Death Penalty Deter Crime?

Finally, we can ask if the death penalty is effective in deterring future crime. Statistics on this can be somewhat difficult to interpret. State-by-state comparisons are notoriously hard to make because of different population demographics that exist among states and because of the different law enforcement standards and procedures that may be in use in different parts of the country. Keeping this in mind, studies have found no clear pattern of differences in murder rates in states with and without the death penalty. Also, studies have revealed no significant drop in murder rates when the death penalty is reinstated in states after a period of time without it. So does the death penalty deter crime? We have little hard evidence that it does (Radelet and Lacock 2009).

What Do We Do with All This Information?

The question, then, becomes, how do we put all of this information together? As we have seen, we can examine the use of the death penalty from a variety of perspectives. First, we can look at this issue from a process point of view, and ask whether the death penalty can ever be implemented with a sufficiently low enough level of bias and inaccuracies to be fair. Second, we can also access it from an outcome standpoint, and question how effective it has to be in deterring crime to be defensible. Third, and perhaps most importantly, we can look at the death penalty from a moral viewpoint, and ask whether its use has an overall good or bad impact on our society. Does it, that is, affirm our core values because it signals how strongly we revere the worth of each victim's life, or does its use tarnish and degrade our moral standing in the world because it shows us to be a somewhat barbaric and unforgiving people. These are the great imponderables.

Applications: Putting This Together to Debate Some Bigger Policy Issues

We have reviewed some of the major research and theories on the topic of retributive justice. We have looked at the purpose of punishment, the meaning of legal guilt and innocence, and the idea of fairness in methods of punishment.

As in previous chapters, in the following section, proposals relevant to each of these different topics will be presented, and then a series of questions will be given. Do not worry about trying to find a right or wrong answer as you work with these questions. Rather simply attempt to bring in as many viewpoints and perspectives as you can to your analyses to spark your ability to think critically about these very important topics.

Retributive Justice Policy Dilemma #1: "Victimless Crimes"

Victimless crimes are crimes in which there is no clear injury inflicted on others, and the only victim involved is the perpetrator of the crime itself. There has been a lot of debate lately about the fairness of sentencing individuals to long-term prison for committing these types of crimes, especially for victimless crimes like illegal drug use. Those who support use of harsh sentencing protocols for such crimes would suggest that these sentences send a clear message to society about the kind of destructive behavior we will not tolerate. Drug use, they would suggest, not only hurts the individual users, but also destroys families and neighborhoods and often leads to other more egregious crimes. According to this viewpoint, if we can signal through our criminal penalty system about our disapproval of drug usage, our society as a whole will be strengthened and individuals will be deterred from start-ing harmful addictive habits.

On the other hand, those who disapprove of harsh sentencing laws for crimes like drug use might argue that victimless crimes hurt only the in-dividual victim and not others in society. Why then, they would suggest, should we not allow individuals to make their own choices about whether to indulge in these types of destructive acts or not, without criminalizing their decisions. People on this side of the debate might also assert that there is hypocrisy here because we allow individuals to overuse substances such as cigarettes, alcohol, sugar, and salt, all of which are known to pose considerable health risks for many people, without the interference of law enforcement. Why not the same for so-called illegal drugs?

Construct arguments in support of both sides of this issue. What po-sition seems most fair to you in an ideal world? Why? When you do this, think of the ideas presented in this chapter about the purpose of punish-ment, notions of guilt, and the fairness of different penalty methods.

Other points to ponder in terms of fairness:

1. Should the type of drug that the individual used be taken into con-sideration when thinking about penalty appropriateness? What fac-tors would you use to assess whether a particular drug should be illegal or not?

2. Should penalties only be given to those who sell drugs to others, not to the drug users themselves? Why or why not?

3. Is there something about the nature of so-called "hard drugs" (e.g., cocaine, heroin) that makes them different from other mind altering

substances that people use such as alcohol? Why should cocaine and heroin drugs be treated differently?

4. How should the fact that these drugs are very addictive be factored into our considerations of their legality or illegality? Is it addiction, itself, which we want to regulate? Should we also outlaw other substances such as tobacco or even chocolate or caffeine that also have addictive qualities? Why or why not?

Retributive Justice Policy Dilemma #2: Death to Terrorists

We have talked about the pros and cons of the use of the death penalty in the United States. One key question is if there is ever a time when its use would be completely justified. That is, are there any types of crimes that are so horrific or so destructive to society that we should not even consider allowing the perpetrators of these crimes to live? To think about this, imagine that two individuals who were affiliated with terrorist groups planted bombs in the New York subway system and caused over 1,000 people to die. The question is what penalty should these two individuals receive to pay for their crime? Should they receive the death penalty or should they be given some lesser sentence in which their life is spared?

Construct arguments in support of both sides of this issue. What position seems most fair to you in an ideal world? Why? When you do this, think of the ideas presented in this chapter about the purpose of punishment, notions of guilt, and the fairness of different penalty methods.

Other points to ponder in terms of fairness:

1. Should the number of people who were killed by these individuals be taken into consideration as you think about this? What, for instance, if only one person was killed? Would that change your ideas about what type of penalty would be most appropriate?

2. Does the fact that these individuals were found to be affiliated with terrorists groups make a difference in your thinking about penalty appropriateness? What if they just acted on their own with no terrorist connections?

3. Would it make any difference to you if you knew that these terrorists were under threat when they committed their act of bombing, and that they were told by their leader that they would be killed themselves if they did not complete their task of placing the bombs in the subway?

4. What if you know that these terrorists were highly religious and were doing what they thought God commanded them to do? Would this change your thinking about penalty appropriateness at all?

Retributive Justice Policy Dilemma #3: A Case of Sex Offenders

There has been much discussion in this country about what to do with people who have committed sex offenses and have served their allotted time in prison for their offenses. In many areas of the country some type of antipredator laws are in place that severely restrict where these ex-offenders may live and work after their release from confinement. These restrictions can run from outlawing living in entire towns to restricting residence in places where children are apt to gather like parks or schools or playgrounds.

Those who support these kinds of antipredator laws point to the fact that their purpose is to protect our children. That, they say, not the burden it may place on the ex-offender, should be our first priority.

Those who are against these kinds of restrictions, on the other hand, feel that antipredator laws unfairly and doubly penalize people who have been convicted of sex offenses and have already paid the price for their crime in prison. They also point out that these types of restrictions severely marginalize individuals and make it harder for them to reenter and work productively in society. This, they suggest, may actually have the effect of increasing rather than decreasing the potential threat that these individuals may pose to others.

Construct arguments in support of both sides of this issue. What position seems most fair to you in an ideal world? Why? When you do this, think of the ideas presented in this chapter about the purposes of punishment, notions of guilt, and the fairness of different penalty methods.

Other points to ponder in terms of fairness:

1. Would it make any difference to you if you knew the offender involved had been arrested for a first offense versus multiple past offenses? Why or why not?
2. Would it make any difference to you if you knew that statistics suggest that the great majority of sex offenses do not occur between strangers and children, but rather are committed by family members or some friend that the child already knew.
3. Would the age of the child victim make any difference to you as you think about the appropriateness of these antipredator laws? What, for instance, if the victim was a 17-year-old girl? Would that be the same in your mind as an offense committed with a 10-year-old child?
4. What if the victim was not a minor, at all, but a consenting adult? For instance, what if, the crime involved consenting adults who were engaging in inappropriate sexual behavior in a public place such as a family beach or park?

Summary

In this chapter a review of the major research findings in the area of retributive justice was presented. Several key themes emerged as we examined this topic. First, the goals of legal punishment are diverse and can include attempting to stop or deter future crime, trying to make good the harm done to the crime victim, reforming the offender, and sending a broader message to society about the types of values we want to affirm.

Second, multiple factors are taken into account when decisions are made about whether a person is deserving of different types of legal punishment. These factors include whether the offender was aware of the consequences of his or her actions when they committed the crime; whether they intended to inflict harm on others or just acted in a careless manner; and whether they had sufficient cognitive capacity to be able to reason about and plan their actions. These factors can be considered both when assessments of guilt or innocence are made, and when decisions about punishment recommendations are put in place.

Just as it is sometimes difficult to determine who should or should not be punished, there also can be controversy around questions about how we should punish others, or what are fair and appropriate penalties for offenders who have violated the law in different ways. Penalties for law violations can range from financial fines to a sentence of death. This last form of punishment by death is one of the most contentious. When we examine its use, we see particular variation across different states. Although some argue that when we sentence someone to death for taking the life of another person we send a powerful affirmative message to society about the value we place on the victim's life, others assert that sentencing anyone to death for any crime is barbaric and amounts to no more than state-sanctioned murder. A more detailed discussion of the topic of retributive justice is provided in Wenzel and Okimoto (2016).

References

Adler, Freda, Gerhard O. Mueller and William S. Laufer. 2009. *Criminality* (6th edition). New York, NY: McGraw-Hill.

Atkins v. Virginia, 536 U.S. 304 (2002).

Bedan, Hugo Adam. 2005. *Debating the Death Penalty: Should America Have Capital Punishment? The Experts on Both Sides Make Their Case.* Oxford, England: Oxford University Press.

Braithwaite, John J. 2007. "Encourage Restorative Justice." *Criminology and Public Policy.* 6 (4): 689–696.

Carlsmith, Kevin M. and John M. Darley. 2008. "Psychological Aspects of Retributive Justice." In *Advances in Experimental Social Psychology,* edited by Mark Zanna, 193–236, New York, NY: Academic Press.

Carlsmith, Kevin M., John M. Darley and Paul H. Robinson. 2002. "Why Do We Punish? Deterrence and Just Deserts as Motives for Punishment." *Journal of Personality and Social Psychology.* 83 (2): 284–299.

Cohen, Ronald L. 2016."Restorative Justice." In *The Handbook of Social Justice Theory and Research,* edited by Clara Sabbagh and Manfred Schmitt, 257–272, New York, NY: Springer.

Costanzo, Mark. 2004. *Psychology Applied to the Law.* Belmont, CA: Wadsworth-Thompson Learning.

Cullen, Francis T., Gregory A. Clark and John F. Wozniak. 1985. "Explaining the Get Tough Movement: Can the Public Be Blamed?" *Federal Probation.* 49 (2): 16–24.

Darley, John M. and Thomas Pittman. 2003. "The Psychology of Compensatory and Retributive Justice." *Personality and Social Psychology Review.* 7: 324–336.

Death Penalty Information Center. 2016. www.deathpenaltyinfo.org.

Digman, James. 2005. *Understanding Victims and Restorative Justice.* Maidenhead, England: Open University Press.

Eaves, Derek, James P. Ogloff and Ronald Roesch, eds. 2000. *Mental Disorders and the Criminal Code: Legal Background and Contemporary Perspectives.* Burnaby, BC: Mental Health Law and Policy Institute, Simon Fraser University.

Fondacaro, Mark, Stephen Koppel, Megan J. O'Toole and Joanne Crain. 2015. "The Rebirth of Rehabilitation in Juvenile and Criminal Justice: New Wine in New Bottles." *Ohio Northern University Law Review: 38th Annual Symposium Articles.* 41: 697–730.

French, Peter A. 2001. *The Virtues of Vengeance.* Lawrence, KS: University of Kansas Press.

Funk, Friederike, Victoria McGeer and Maria Gollwitzer. 2014. "Get the Message: Punishment is Satisfying if the Transgressor Responds to Its Communicative Intent." *Personality and Social Psychology Bulletin.* 40: 986–997.

Furman v. Georgia, 408 U.S. 238 (1972).

Gibbs, Jack P. 1968. "Crime, Punishment and Deterrence." *Southwestern Social Science Quarterly.* 48 (4): 515–530.

Gregg v. Georgia 428 U.S. 153 (1976).

Greene, Edith and Kirk Heilbrun. 2011. *Wrightsman's Psychology and the Legal System* (7th edition). Belmont, CA: Wadsworth-Thompson Learning.

Kaufman, Arnold S. 1960. "The Reform Theory of Punishment." *Ethics.* 71 (1): 49–53.

Nagin, Daniel S. 1998. "Deterrence and Incapacitation." In *The Handbook of Crime and Punishment,* edited by Michael Tonry, 345–368. New York, NY: Oxford University Press.

Palmetti, Nicholas M. and Jennifer P. Russo, eds. 2011. *Psychology of Punishment.* New York, NY: Nova Science Publishers, Inc.

Poulson, Ronald, Karl L. Wuensch and Michael Brondino. 1998. "Factors That Discriminate Among Mock Jurors' Verdict Selection: Impact of Guilty but Mentally Ill Verdict Option." *Criminal Justice and Behavior.* 25 (3): 366–381.

Radelet, Michael and Traci T. Lacock. 2009. "Do Executions Lower Homicide Rates? The Views of Leading Criminologists." *Journal of Criminal Law and Criminology.* 99 (2): 489–508.

Roper v. Simmons 543 U.S. 551 (2005).

Smith, Robert J. 2011. "The Geography of the Death Penalty and Its Ramifications." *Boston University Law Review.* August 22.

Slobogin, Christopher, Thomas Hafemeister, Douglass Mossman and Ralph Reisner. 2013. *Law and the Mental Health System: Civil and Criminal Aspects* (6th edition). St. Paul, MN: West Academic Publishing, American Casebook Series.

Strang, Heather. 2002. *Repair or Revenge: Victims and Restorative Justice.* Oxford, England: Clarendon Press.

The Innocence Project. 2016. www.innocenceproject.org.

Tversky, Amos and Daniel Kahneman. 1974. "Judgment under Uncertainty: Heuristics and Biases." *Science.* 185 (4157): 1124–1131.

Vidmar, Neil and Dale T. Miller. 1980. "The Social Psychology of Punishment." *Law and Society Review.* 14: 565–602.

Wenzel, Michael, Tyler G. Okimoto, Norman T. Feather and Michael J. Platow. 2008. "Retributive and Restorative Justice." *Law and Human Behavior.* 32: 375–389.

Wenzel, Michael, Tyler G. Okimoto. 2016. "Retributive Justice." in *The Handbook of Social Justice Theory and Research,* 237–256, New York, NY: Springer.

CHAPTER 4

Societal Justice

Abstract

In this chapter a review of what is sometimes called "societal justice" is presented. This term is used to denote ideas about human rights and the relationship that exists between individuals and the larger, governing state. Major headings in this chapter are human rights and the Universal Declaration, the nature of human rights, the question of rights' universality, rights and power, and the impact of rights documents. Each of these major headings is further divided into subsections.

Particular attention is paid to an examination of the Universal Declaration of Human Rights, which was written in 1948 shortly after the end of World War II (The United Nations 1948). This document set a framework in place for many other subsequent rights documents and was used to inform significant aspects of international rights law. Topics examined will include a discussion of what types of things should be considered rights versus privileges; the question of the universality versus the culturally relative nature of rights; and the issue of who should determine what is or is not a right, for whom, and in what context.

Definition of Societal Justice

In the previous chapters we examined three different models of social justice. We asked questions such as "Were resources distributed to individuals in society in a fair manner?" "Were the procedures in place to make decisions about individuals fair?" and "Was punishment allocated justly to those who committed offenses?"

In this chapter we will examine another type of justice that conceptualizes fairness a bit differently. We are going to call this "societal justice."

Societal justice is concerned with broad ideas about human rights, and with the relationships that exist between the individual and the larger state or nation. To start thinking about this topic we might consider a number of issues. First, we can reflect on what type of rights, if any, we think individuals should possess simply by virtue of being human. Second, we can ask ourselves whether we believe human rights are universal, or if they are better thought of as being particular to different situational contexts and cultural circumstances. Third, we can ponder what kind of state we think would exist if the human rights of all citizens were fully protected, and if such a state is even possible. And finally, and perhaps most importantly, we can ask who should get to decide who and what should be protected under the rubric of human rights.

Human Rights and the Universal Declaration

The nature of human rights, of course, has been debated by scholars, philosophers, and religious leaders throughout history. Here we are going to examine a specific way of thinking about these rights that emerged during the French Enlightenment period in the 18th century. This view sees human rights resting mainly on secular, not religious, contracts between the people and their leaders (Hayden 2001). An example of this Enlightenment outlook on rights can be found in an important human rights document called the *Universal Declaration of Human Rights* (UDHR) (Hayden 2001). The structure presented in that document will serve as the main framework that we will use for thinking about human rights in this chapter. The conceptualization of rights presented in this declaration is particularly important because it is one of the first documents of its type to be signed by representatives from multiple nations of the world, and it is one of the few declarations in which the human rights were not just abstractly described, but rather were spelled out in very specific, practical terms.

The UDHR document was written just after hostilities in World War II had ended. As a result of this war, millions and millions of people had been killed or wounded, and much of Europe and parts of Asia and African had been destroyed. The scope of the holocaust had been uncovered. The question on the minds of many was how to form a new kind of world order so that this type of large-scale destruction would be less apt to occur again. In part because of this concern, the United Nations was founded in 1945; it brought 48 countries of the world together in a multinational forum. A Human Rights Commission consisting of 18 individuals from different countries was then created within this new UN structure, and commission members were given the task of defining what types of basic rights all human beings should possess in fair and just societies (Humphrey 1979). Commission members worked tediously for 2 years to craft the specific language that resulted in the UDHR document. Since this declaration was written, other documents have been produced that further codify the social, cultural, economic, and political rights outlined in the UDHR (The United Nations 1966a; 1966b) and that guarantee human rights to particular groups such as women and children (The United Nations 1979; 1989). However, our main attention here will be on the original UDHR framework. Our goal is not to critique or evaluate this document, or even to review its provisions in any detail. Rather, we will use it as a conceptual guide to start thinking about what we mean when we say all humans deserve a certain measure of human rights. What types of rights are we talking about? Is it reasonable, as the writers of the declaration attempted to do, to assert that these rights should exist for all human beings, regardless of culture or context? Are economic and social rights as basic to human beings as broader civic and political rights? Can we define human rights at all, or is the whole attempt to do so just a futile philosophical exercise with no real world consequences? Let's take a look at some of these questions.

The Nature of Human Rights: What Kind of Rights Are We Talking About?

The Key Idea of Dignity

The rights outlined in the UDHR and other UN rights documents rest on the central idea of the inherent dignity of all human life (Howard 1992). It is from this key premise that all of the rights contained in them flow. But what is this illusive concept of dignity? What does it mean to have it or not have it? And can a state provide it? The writers of these documents, in fact, felt that by the promotion of certain practices and policies, the state or nation could enhance the nature of the human experience. The various documents present templates on how to structure environments that promote human flourishing. The rights that are addressed emphasize the necessity of non discrimination for all people, and the importance of freedom and personal autonomy of action. The focus is on the worth of the individual actor, and his or her ability to construct a life of meaning and self-fulfillment (Bietz 2001).

What Is the State Morally Obligated to Do and Not to Do?

In the original UDHR framework, 30 different articles were included that addressed different types of universal human rights. Many of the rights defined are negative, but a few positive rights are enumerated as well. Positive rights are probably the type of rights that first come to mind when we think of human rights. These are rights *to* something. They oblige state action (Centre for Constitutional Studies 2013). We might think, for example, that a civilized state has a moral obligation to provide all its citizens with a certain minimum standard of living in terms of such things as sufficient food for survival or decent shelter for housing. Positive rights can also be defined in terms of certain guarantees for certain types of processes such as access to public hearings for those accused of crimes. These types of positive rights represent notions of what the state should be morally bound to provide for all of its citizens, not as a favor or because of particular merit on the part of the citizens, but simply because all humans deserve these rights. This way of conceptualizing deservingness, it might be noted, is more democratic and nondifferentiating among individuals than the models of deservingness that we discussed in the first chapter of this book where we considered distributive justice.

To help us think about this a bit more we can consider an example of an individual named Jennifer who enjoys the right to a free basic education in some country of the world. The framers of these human rights documents would say that Jennifer should be guaranteed this right not because she did anything to earn this, but simply because it is her birthright. Establishing something as a right equalizes power between the rights' giver and the rights' receiver. Jennifer should not feel indebted in any way to the giver of the right (the state in this case) because what was provided was simply her due. The state, in turn, also should not use the allocation of these types of rights to reward some and punish others since they should be granted to everyone without exception. This is quite a radical notion! Of course, it is easier to assert general agreement with these types of abstract ideas than to put them into place in actual practice.

Human rights as exemplified in these types of UN documents can additionally be conceptualized in a negative manner. These types of rights are rights *from* something happening to an individual, and they specify things the state should have a moral obligation *not* to do in a civilized society (Centre for Constitutionalist Studies 2013). For instance, we might believe that everyone should have a right not to be subject to arbitrary arrest or to torture by the state, or not to be impeded from freely practicing the religion of their choice. These rights should be guaranteed to all without exceptions. For instance, I should refrain from torturing you not because you are a particularly nice or a worthy person, but because all individuals deserve some level of humane treatment from others.

Again, we can see that guaranteeing these types of negative rights may be easier to state abstractly than to put in place at a more concrete, specific level. One problem is how to operationalize terms like torture. Is it torture, for instance, to waterboard someone to extract information from them? Should there be any exceptions to this rule of never using torture? Is a definition of torture in one culture apt to be the same as the definition in another culture? These are some of the complicating considerations that can make straightforward implementation of these types of negative guarantees practically difficult.

Thinking About Food versus Freedom

In addition to affirming both positive and negative human rights, the writers of these universal rights documents also made distinctions between rights based more on process factors versus those focused more on outcomes (Patman 2000). Rights of access to certain processes tend to be in the political, civic, spiritual, or cultural domain. An example of a process right would be the right to freedom of assembly.

Outcome rights, on the other hand, guarantee access to more concrete types of benefits. These tend to be more social or economic in nature. Examples of these rights would be things like rights to decent pay for work, or to sufficient food and affordable shelter.

Although the framers of these documents equally valued both outcome and process rights, in some areas of the world more or less emphasis is placed on one or the other of these. For instance, in many Western cultures basic human rights tend to be defined more in terms of civic and political freedoms than economic and social rights. The idea here is not that social and economic benefits are unimportant, but rather that they can best be promoted if these civic and political rights are first protected. Thus, individuals might be granted the right to pursue wealth and an adequate standard of living, but the outcome of this pursuit might not be guaranteed. This is the language, for instance, that is used in the American Declaration of Independence.

In some other areas of the world, human rights are construed more in terms of tangible resources that the state should provide its citizens. Here we would say that individuals do not merely have the right to *pursue* a certain level of health care or an adequate standard of living, but rather, that the state has a moral obligation to provide these benefits to its citizens as their due. These social and economic rights are seen as being fundamental and basic to a just society, and they are considered preconditions to any other types of rights.

Of course, in most cultures some mix of both of these civic/political/spiritual and economic/social types of rights are represented. The issue is often just where the degree of emphasis is placed. Also, how we think about all of this tends to be deeply culturally embedded. We might imagine, for instance, a young man who has grown up in a society called Society Y where civic and political freedoms are strongly emphasized. Perhaps this young man visits a culture called Society X where these freedoms are very restricted. For instance, in Society X people are not allowed free access to information, they are not allowed to express their ideas about the state openly and honestly, and they are not allowed to gather in public places to protest any aspects of their condition. This all might seem horrible and intolerable to the young man from Society Y. Interestingly, however, perhaps many of the citizens in Society X tell this young man that in their society they are treated very justly. The state, they assert, guarantees everyone such things a right to free health care, education, child care, maternity leave, and adequate food and shelter. When they hear about the young man's culture, they are somewhat appalled by what they hear. They point out the tremendous discrepancies between wealth and poverty that exist there, the number of people living on the streets without shelter, the high crime and divorce rates, and the number of children that who do not have adequate child care. Who is right here? This can be difficult to judge.

Rights versus Duties and Religious Obligations

We have seen how the way basic human rights are conceptualized can vary in different cultural and political situations. Also, people in different cultures can differ on whether or not individual rights are even seen as important to the creation of a just society. The "rights centric" view is very in line with values endorsed in the United States and other Western cultures where the focus tends to be on removing restraints that may stand in the way of a personal pursuit of happiness. Here the assumption is that people do best when they are given maximum opportunity to make their own choices and act on their own desires (Pollis and Schwab 1980). In this framework, duty and obligations to others, even to family, are seen as being fairly discretionary and not morally imperative. For example, it is good to be nice to your parents in their old age, but it is not required. Often, in fact, there may be a slight inherent tension between balancing duty and achieving maximal self or individual fulfillment. For instance, if I spend too much time caring for my family, how can my ability to fulfill my own potential be maximized?

In other societies the situation may be very, very different. An alternative viewpoint to the individualism that we have described above is that people exist not to fulfill themselves, but rather to serve the greater good, which is defined by one's family or clan or society as a whole (Jacobson and Bruun 2000; Meijer 2001). In some places of the world, in fact, a word for the notion of individual human "rights" does not even exist as we understand the term in the West (de Benoist 2011). Rather, we would speak more of human obligations defined as the ability to fulfill competently one's duties and roles in society. These duties and roles consist of moral obligations to others, especially the extended family, and they are not discretionary. For instance, in these societies I would not choose to help my aging father because I may want to be a nice person or because I may feel sorry for his suffering. Rather, I would do this because it is a requirement of my role as a good daughter. Interestingly, in the 30 articles of the original UDHR framework only 1 article enumerated the types of duties and obligations that should be required of individuals in a just state. Some see this as an example of Western bias in the document itself.

A second alternative viewpoint to the Western individualistic, secular model is to assert that all human rights should flow from religious prescriptions. These prescriptions should be seen as nonnegotiable and binding, and as a central core of any rights discussion. Religious belief here is not seen as a right to be chosen or not chosen, but rather as a necessary foundational structure that underlies all justice thinking (Baderin 2003; Mayer 2007).

These represent very different worldviews and give rise to very different understandings of human rights and justice. Dissatisfaction with what some people saw as the cultural limits of the original UDHR documents, in fact, led to the creation of several other declarations that the writers thought better reflected regional cultural concerns. One of these was the Bangkok Declaration that was written to represent more Asian views of human rights (UN Regional Asia Pacific World Conference on Human Rights 1993). And, in 2000, several Islamic countries came together to write what was called the "Cairo Declaration of Human Rights" in which it was declared that people should have certain kinds of rights guaranteed only if these rights are found to be in accordance with Shari'ah law (Organisation of the Islamic Cooperation 1990).

Thus, deep cultural disagreements can and do exist over the way that a just life is defined, and over conceptions of the appropriate role of society in promoting such a life. What basic rights may seem obvious to one cultural group may seem peripheral or even unsuitable to another.

Focus on Me versus Focus on My Group

We have seen that when we talk about a just society, the focus can be on the individual standing alone or the individual embedded within the group.

Let's talk more about this notion of group rights and how it may differ from conceptualizations of individuals' rights (Jones 1999; Triggs 1988).

To think about this, we might imagine a young girl who is a member of some hypothetical tribe in a certain part of the world. This young girl has been raised according to the traditions of her village. Part of these traditions demand that she becomes a bride at the age of 12 or 13 years old to an older man of her parents' choosing. If she does not marry at this age the chances are high that she will never be deemed a suitable bride for anyone. As you consider this, further imagine that a human rights health worker from some Western country visits this village and talks to the villagers about the health risks that young girls face when they marry so early. She discusses the higher rate of complications from pregnancy when one is so young, and the higher numbers of childbirth deaths that may occur. In order to try to start somewhere to change the villagers' marriage practices, this rights worker then talks to the parents of a young girl who is scheduled to be married the next week. The human rights worker urges this girl's parents to stop the wedding. When they refuse, the worker laments the backward state of their thinking and their selfish inability to focus on their daughter's needs and rights.

We can look at the above as an illustration of a clash between the individual rights of the daughter and the group rights of this tribe. Which rights should be privileged? Should the young girl's individual well-being outweigh decades of tradition in this tribe? What if this tribe existed as a sort of minority group in the midst of a state that had different ideas about raising children and marriage? Would it be just for this majority state to dictate how this tribe should handle their marriage arrangements, or should the tribe's beliefs and practices be protected?

As we think about this we have to consider what we are trying to do when we honor different types of rights (Melton 2008). It is easy to think about why we place so much importance on individual rights. We cherish these rights because we want to enhance a person's human dignity and ability to live unrestricted and self-directed lives. But what do we enhance when we protect group rights? Are not group affiliations and traditions, moral codes and rituals also an important part of individual identity? Wouldn't the young girl in the case discussed above lose an essential connection to her tribe, and her sense of worth and security that flows from that if she individually defied the tribe's marriage traditions? These are not easy questions to answer, and we will come back to them later in this chapter. For now, suffice it to say that sometimes individual and group rights clash, and favoring one can sometimes have deleterious effects on the other.

Are Any Rights Universal?

A key question underlying all of the previous discussion is whether *any* types of rights are truly universal and apply equally in all cultures and contexts, or whether all rights are culturally relative in nature. This can be complicated to determine. Perhaps, for instance, someone suggests that certainly some rights such as the right to not have physical pain inflicted unjustly on us are so basic that they should be protected for people everywhere. This seems to be a fairly straightforward proposition that would be difficult to argue against. The problem comes, however, when we try to define what we mean by unjust infliction of pain. We might imagine a culture which had a tradition of foot binding for women, as China did in the past. Or maybe in some society various types of body piercing and physical scarring are deemed to be necessary for achievement of cultural standards of beauty. Would these practices, if culturally promoted and, in fact, deemed necessary, involve a violation of an individual's rights to health and bodily integrity, or should we see them simply as cultural practices that we ought to protect? This is the gist of the cultural universalism versus cultural relativism dilemma. Let's think about this some more by arguing for both sides of these ideas.

It Is All in the Eye of the Beholder

Those who argue for a culturally relativist perspective would say that all types of cultural practices, even those we personally find to be repugnant, should be interpreted in light of the prevailing cultural traditions in place within the societies in which they occur. Furthermore, cultural relativists would add that we cannot competently judge practices in other cultures because, as outsiders, we can never achieve full understanding of the context in which they take place (Ignatieff 2001; Renteln 1985).

Consider again the old Chinese custom of foot binding. This custom had a long and complex evolution and, when it was practiced in China, it was embedded within many other types of norms and role obligations for women. Although it may have seemed abhorrent to some Western eyes, it was defined quite differently at the time that it took place in China. So the question becomes who are we to judge? Is it fair to judge anything at all if we risk doing so ignorantly and without full understanding? Would we think it appropriate to have others judge us? For instance, we might ask how outsiders might view some of our own culturally promoted practices to improve appearance such as tattooing, ear or lip piercing, or use of plastic surgery. What about implementation of the death penalty as a form of punishment for some crimes? Can others morally evaluate these types of practices if they do not completely comprehend the cultural environment in which these practices take place? Those who ascribe to the morally relativist viewpoint would say they cannot.

Some Practices Are Just Bad Everywhere

Of course, there is another side to this argument. Some would suggest that cultural relativism should have some limits, and that some practices of the world, even if they are sanctioned by cultural traditions, are so objectionable that we should define them being unjust in any context (Mahoney 2007). If foot binding, for instance, was found to cause great pain and disfigurement, it should be seen as wrong and a violation of human rights in any culture. If one concluded that capital punishment produces intolerable suffering in individuals, it should be considered inhumanly cruel regardless of any cultural beliefs that might exist that support its use. This type of cultural absolutism position, thus, asserts that we can objectively analyze the characteristics of practices outside of their situational circumstances. The "rub," though, is how to determine the exact standards we should use to do this. What is intolerable pain? What type of caused suffering should we protect against? Does the infliction of pain on another always consist of a type of rights denial, or can it ever be justified? When, for that matter, does cultural context matter and when does it not matter?

Rights and Power

We have examined how human rights can be viewed from multiple perspectives by both individuals from within and from outside different types of cultural environments. But how might the way that power is distributed among people in societies affect how we think about what should and should not be considered a rights violation (Binion 1995; Qureshi 2012)? What if, for example, we found that some cultural norms and traditions that we protect were mainly put in place by one group within a culture at the expense of others? We might imagine, for instance, that certain female dress codes and travel restrictions that we observed in a particular culture were put in place not by the women who were directly affected by them, but rather by men in the society to guard their own status and power. Should this matter to us as we think about how and if these women's rights had been abused? Should we be especially sensitive to customs that seem to privilege some groups and not others? These types of issues can make our ability to render morally sound judgments of the cultural traditions of others even more complicated.

Looking Again at Rights Documents

We started this discussion of human rights by talking about certain documents on human rights that were written after the end of World War II. The framers of these documents wrote them with the intention of positively impacting the lives of people throughout the world. The rights they laid out were declared to be universal and nonnegotiable. In a just society, the framers asserted that these rights should be promoted and protected. But how much impact have these types of documents actually had? There is a debate about this. Some suggest that the impact has been minimal, in part, because the documents themselves were nonbinding, and the nations that signed them were not required to agree to any standard way to monitor compliance. Without this enforcement ability, it can be argued that these documents become merely words on paper. Others, however, say that even without strict enforcement capability, these types of rights documents are important. They are important because they can help set a stage for dialogue about the nature of human rights. They provide a framework from which international law can draw. More importantly they set a tone and provide a vision of what a just and humane society might look like (Donnelly 2013). This last point takes us back to the question of whether there can be any one vision of societal justice that fits all. Are the "universal" rights talked about in documents like the UDHR truly universal? Can rights be defined outside of the religious, cultural, and moral context in which they are embedded? These questions are not likely to be resolved soon, if ever.

Applications: Putting This Together to Debate Some Bigger Policy Issues

We have reviewed some of the ideas about how to consider the nature of human rights. Now, as in previous chapters, you will be given the chance to use the information presented in this chapter to critically analyze some policy issues pertinent to human rights concerns. There are many such concerns. For example, how should we deal with practices in other cultures that we personally find to be degrading and disgusting and violating of individuals' basic human rights? Can we condemn them without inappropriately imposing on others our own values and sense of right and wrong? How do we decide what is a right in society and what is a privilege? Should economic benefits and social services be considered rights? If so, what kinds of services and benefits, and what standard do we use to decide? And finally, how do we remain sensitive to the importance of group cultural customs and traditions while still supporting freedom of individual choice and initiative? Is this particularly a concern when the groups in question are minority groups who have historically struggled to retain their cultural identity as a people? These are some of the issues we will deal with in this last section of the chapter.

As we have done in previous chapters, ideas and proposals pertaining to some of these issues will be presented, followed by a series of questions. These questions have no clear right or wrong answers. Rather they are included to help you think more critically about these types of human rights dilemmas, and to enable you to view arguments about them from multiple perspectives.

Major Human Rights Dilemma #1: The Case of Female Circumcision

In some countries of the world, young girls are required to have a circumcision procedure (cutting off of the clitoris of the female genitals) take place before they are considered to be eligible for marriage. This is viewed as a sort of rite of passage for girls, and it is often carried out by some of the older women in the community. One purpose of this is to control a woman's sexuality by making sex less pleasurable. Complications from the procedure can be fairly common, especially if it is done without the use of sterile and sanitized instruments. There has been considerable debate from individuals about the moral efficacy of this practice, particularly among those who advocate for human rights for women. Some suggest that because circumcision subjects young girls to great pain and potential long-term suffering, it should be outlawed wherever it takes place around the world. In this view, female circumcision rituals represent a violation of young girls' basic human rights. This is particularly so since in most cases where it is used, young girls often have no choice about whether to have or not have the procedure. It is simply imposed on them.

Others would say that we must be careful about condemning procedures like female circumcision because we may not fully understand the context in which they may take place or the reasons that these practices were initiated in the first place. People also point to inconsistencies in individuals' outrage. For example, are we as concerned about circumcision rituals carried out on young boy babies, as take place in many regions of the world, including the United States? What if other rites of passage rituals that may exist such as body piercing or scarring or burning that may be required practices in some cultural groups? What defines something which should be seen as "wrong" and universally condemned versus something that may be tolerated in the name of cultural diversity? That is the key question.

Construct arguments in support of both sides of this issue. What position seems most fair to you in an ideal world? Why?

1. Should the degree of suffering that the young girls undergo when they have this procedure be the main factor that should be taken into account when deciding if the practice should be universally condemned?

Would it be okay if it was carried out under sedation in controlled conditions in modern medical facilities?

2. Does the fact that the girls who undergo this procedure usually have no choice in the matter make a difference to you as you evaluate whether its use represents a violation of the young girls rights? What if girls could opt to have or not have this done? Would that somehow make the practice more acceptable?

3. Would knowledge that these customs often originated from the dictates of male leaders about the types of young girls who should be eligible for marriage affect how you view this practice? Would you think differently if you thought that it evolved in societies in which women, not men, held most positions of power?

4. Can you think of any circumstances in which this type of practice should be allowed without reservation? What would be the nature of these circumstances?

Major Human Rights Dilemma #2: Human Rights in "Prego"

Imagine a debate taking place about a hypothetical country named "Prego." In this country a revolution just occurred, and the previous democratic leader was replaced by a military dictator. During the earlier regime, people were guaranteed rights to vote, to practice the religion of their choice, to freely express themselves, and to openly gather in public places. Now these rights have been taken away. Access to information is restricted and people are allowed to have no voice in government processes. Freedom of religion is also not tolerated, and individuals now have no rights of free assembly. However, the people now have greater access to a range of government services and resources. Before the revolution, the people of Prego were very poor. Many individuals were homeless and starving in the streets. Medical care was available only for the very rich, and most children were uneducated. Under the new dictatorship all of this has changed. "Pregans" now are provided free housing and medical care. Children can go to public schools where nutritional meals are given to them. All individuals are encouraged to work, and free child care is provided when parents are away from the home.

Your task as a human rights worker is to analyze the human rights situation as it exists now in Prego. Is Prego a better place since the revolution?

Are the people's lives "improved?" Are there more or less human rights violations taking place since the revolutionaries took over?

Construct arguments in support of both sides of this issue. What position seems most fair to you in an ideal world? Why?

1. Would it make a difference if you knew that statistics in Prego show that infant mortality and malnutrition rates have significantly decreased since the revolution, and that literacy rates have significantly increased? Why or why not?

2. What if opinion polls showed that the people of Prego are actually happier now post revolution than they were before the revolution? Should that matter in your assessment of the human right situation there?

3. What if you were told that people have been murdered by the government in Prego for trying to speak out about their lack of freedom? Would this impact your thinking about the human rights situation there? What if the murdered people represented only a very small number of the people who live in Prego?

4. Would you think differently about this if you used a long-term versus a short-term perspective to consider what type of state you wanted to permanently promote for the Pregan people?

*Major Allocation Dilemma # 3: Human Rights
and Integrated Schooling*

In the United States we have a very diverse culture consisting of people of different races and religions and ethnic backgrounds. A challenge that can exist in these types of diverse environments is how to put policies in place that allow individuals to maintain and honor their rich and unique cultural traditions without isolating themselves from the benefits of full participation in the larger culture. To think about this a bit more, imagine a situation in which Native Americans in some community in the American West ran schools for their own children. In these schools the children were taught about their heritage and history. They were also taught to speak their own tribal language and to understand their ancestors' religious traditions. Only Native Americans could attend these schools, and consequently the children who went to them had very little contact with the nonnative community in the larger culture. Some people felt that these schools worked to put the Native American children at a disadvantage when, as young adults, they tried to find jobs in the mainstream culture. Because they had been so isolated and had so few social contacts with those outside their own group, it was quite hard for them to leave their own communities.

Imagine now that as a remedy to this, some people proposed that the Native American children should be moved from their tribal schools and placed in public educational institutions outside their communities. They would be given new nonnative names like Jack or Jennifer and they would have full access to all of the schools' instructional resources. Even more importantly, they would be able to make friends and bond with students, teachers, and other mentors at these schools who could help them later in life to integrate into the mainstream culture.

The question is whether the above "integration proposal" is a good idea. Would being forced to attend these public schools enhance these children's lives by giving them a right to an educational experience that would benefit them later, or would it harm them and be a violation of their rights in some manner?

Construct arguments in support of both sides of this issue. What position seems most fair to you in an ideal world? Why?

1. Would it make a difference in how you think about this if you knew that the parents and/or the Native American students themselves could choose whether or not to attend these types of public schools? Why or why not?

2. What if statistics showed that the Native American children who did attend these types of public schools were able to secure significantly higher paying jobs after graduation than the children who stayed in the traditional tribal schools? Should this fact be important as you think about this?

3. What if we learned that if these policies were put in place that over time the number of individuals who would be able to speak the old tribal language and who remembered the old traditional religious practices would be significantly diminished? How should this be taken into account as we try to decide if any rights have been violated by this integration policy?

Summary

In this chapter a review of "societal justice" or the relationship that should exist between the individual and the larger state was presented. The framework we used here is based, in part, on a secular notion of human rights that emerged during the period of the French Enlightenment. Particular attention was paid to a document called the *Universal Declaration of Human Rights* that was written after the end of World War II. In this document, which was signed by multiple nations of the world, an Enlightenment view on the types of universal rights that should be protected in just and civilized states is presented. Although it has had considerable impact on how human rights are thought about, some scholars have criticized it as being overly Western in tone, and not truly universal in character.

Rights can vary on numerous dimensions. Some rights specify things that the state must do in a just society, and others specify things the state must refrain from doing. Rights can also address different economic, social, political, civic, religious, and cultural life domains. Rights that the state should guarantee to all its citizens can emphasize tangible outcomes, such as adequate food and shelter, and/or types of participatory processes, such as the right to assemble in public places. Each of these different kinds of rights can be more or less stressed in different types of governing structures, and great debates have taken place on which type are the most essential component of a just society. Some, in fact, have questioned the centrality of individual human rights at all to conceptions of societal justice. Alternatives to this rights-based model of justice emphasize the importance of individuals' fulfillment of duties and obligations to others, or of the fundamental place of religious prescriptions for a moral life.

Group rights can also be distinguished from individual rights. Group rights emphasize the importance of the individual embedded in the larger whole, as opposed to the individual standing alone. These rights consist of guarantees to groups to protect and uphold the traditions, moral codes and rituals that sustain them and contribute to their heritage and identity.

A key question in all of this is whether any human rights are truly universal, or if all are bound to certain unique cultural situations. Those who support a culturally relativist perspective would say that all rights must be viewed and evaluated in terms of the context in which they are practiced. Proponents of a more absolutist position would disagree and say that some rights transcend all cultural boundaries and are universal in nature.

Finally, an issue can be raised about the impact that these attempts to formally codify our understanding of universal human rights have actually had on the lives of individuals around the world. Some would suggest that because the enforcement mechanisms for these types of rights documents are not strong, their impact has been minimal. Others would assert that, to the contrary, attempting to define human rights in a formal way sets the stage for important dialogues about the meaning of justice at a global level.

References

Baderin, Meshood. 2003. *International Human Rights and Islamic Law*. Oxford, England: Oxford Oxford University Press.

Bietz, Charles. 2001. "Human Rights as Common Concerns." *American Political Science Review*. 95 (2): 269–282.

Binion, Gayle. 1995. "Human Rights: A Feminist Perspective." *Human Rights Quarterly*. 17 (3): 509–525.

Centre for Constitutional Studies. 2013. *Positive and Negative Rights*. Canada: University of Alberta.

de Benoist, Alain. 2011. *Beyond Human Rights: Defending Freedoms*. Artkos Media Ltd.

Donnelly, Jack. 2013. *Universal Human Rights in Theory and Practice* (3rd edition). Ithaca, NY: Cornell University Press.

Hayden, Patrick. eds. 2001. *The Philosophy of Human Rights*. St. Paul, MN: Paragon House.

Howard, Rhoda E. 1992. "Dignity, Community and Human Rights." In *Human Rights in Cross-cultural Perspectives: A Quest for Consensus*, edited by Abdullahi Ahmed An-Na'im, 81–102. Philadelphia, PA: University of Pennsylvania Press.

Humphrey, John P. 1979. "The Universal Declaration of Human Rights: Its History, Impact and Juridical Character." In *Human Rights: Thirty Years after the Universal Declaration*, edited by Bertrand G. Ramcharen, 221–237. Leiden, The Netherlands: Brill Publishing.

Ignatieff, Michael. 2001. "The Attack on Human Rights." *Foreign Affairs*. 80: 1–2.

Jacobson, Michael and Ole Bruun, eds. 2000. *Human Rights and Asian Values: Contesting National Identities and Cultural Representations in Asia*. Richmond, Surrey, England: Curzon Press.

Jones, Peter. 1999. "Human Rights, Group Rights and People's Rights." *Human Rights Quarterly.* 21 (1): 80–107.

Mahoney, Jack. 2007. *The Challenge of Human Rights: Origin, Development, and Significance*. Malden, Mass.: Blackwell Publishing Ltd.

Mayer, Ann Elizabeth. 2007. *Islam and Human Rights: Traditions and Politics* (4th edition). Boulder, CO: Westview Press.

Meijer, Martha. eds. 2001. *Dealing with Human Rights: Asian and Western Views on the Value of Human Rights*. Bloomfield, CT: Kumarian Press.

Melton, Gary. 2008. "Beyond Balancing: Toward an Integrated Approach to Children's Rights." *Journal of Social Issues.* 64 (4): 903–920.

Organisation of the Islamic Cooperation. August 5th, 1990. The Cairo Declaration of Human Rights.

Patman, Robert G. eds. 2000. *A Review of Universal Human Rights*. NewYork, NY: St. Martin's Press.

Pollis, Adamantia and Peter Schwab. eds. 1980. *Human Rights: Cultural and Ideological Perspectives*. Santa Barbara, CA: Praeger Publications.

Qureshi, Shazia. 2012. "Feminist Analysis of Human Rights." *Journal of Political Studies.* 19 (2): 41–55.

Renteln, Alison. 1985. "The Unanswered Challenge of Relativism and the Consequences for Human Rights." *Human Rights Quarterly.* 7 (4): 514–540.

The United Nations. 1948. *The Universal Declaration of Human Rights*.

The United Nations. 1966a. *International Covenant on Civil and Political Rights*.

The United Nations. 1966b. *International Covenant on Economic, Social and Cultural Rights*.

The United Nations. 1979. *Convention on the Elimination of All Forms of Discrimination Against Women*.

The United Nations. 1989. *The Convention on the Rights of the Child*.

Triggs, Gillian. 1988. "The Rights of 'Peoples' and Individual Rights: Conflict or Harmony?" In *The Rights of Peoples,* edited by James Crawford, 141–157. Oxford, England: Clarendon Press.

UN Regional Asia Pacific World Conference on Human Rights. April 1993. The Bangkok Declaration of Human Rights.

Summary

Putting It All Together

We have examined social justice from multiple perspectives, and we have seen how complicated considerations of fairness can be. As we think about what we have discussed in this book so far, we might imagine that we are talking with a group of friends who are nearing the end of their lives and taking stock of their experiences. Someone asks the burning question of whether we think we were all treated fairly in life. How we frame this question will have a big impact on our answers (Sabbagh and Schmitt 2016).

What Type of Fairness Are We Talking About?

My Just Due

Three of our friends, Sam, Juliet, and Tiffany, suggest that the most important issue to them is whether they received their fair share of things or resources in their lives. That is, did they obtain the amount of money and the number of goods and services that they felt they were entitled to? When they raise this question, they assert that they are not inquiring whether they received all they wanted or all that they desired to make them happy. Rather, they say they are simply wondering if they obtained in their lives all that they deserved. How they answer this question will have a big influence on their overall sense of worth and life satisfaction, but it sometimes is not an easy determination to make.

First, they would have to deal with the question of how their fair share should be defined. Sam suggests that to him fair share means that the resources he received in his life should have been proportionate to his merit or his level of contributions to society. Imagine that as he thinks back on this he decides he was a bit under-rewarded for all that he did. He remembers working hard to invent new technology tools and software programs that would make life easier for many people, but receiving little to no recognition for these efforts.

Does this sound as if Sam's life was unfair? Who should get to decide what counts and what does not count as merit? Should effort matter in Sam's calculations or only his objective achievements? How should he deal with the possibility of self-interest coloring his own assessments of his own worth? All these considerations would make Sam's assessment of his life fairness less than straightforward.

Imagine now that Juliet too starts to reflect on her life story and the degree to which she received that which she deserved. When she thinks back on this she also feels, similar to Sam, that she came up a bit short. However, the criterion Juliet uses to define deservingness is different than Sam's. Juliet feels that getting her fair share meant getting resources that were proportionate to her needs, not to her contributions. She remembers being very sickly all of her life and requiring a certain level of medical care and support which she felt that she did not obtain. Because of this, she recalls undergoing great suffering, which left her feeling neglected and angry. This, she suggests, was very unfair.

Is Juliet's life story more unfair than Sam's? Who should decide? How do we objectively calculate the level of need and whose need is greater than whose? We end up once again at the "what counts" problem that we had with Sam.

Our third friend, Tiffany, who has been listening to all of this, tries to use an easier way of thinking about it than either Sam or Juliet. Rather, she states that she simply wanted to receive as much as others did, not more or not less. That would be fair to her. But when she starts to consider this more deeply she begins to run into trouble. Who exactly should she compare herself to? On what dimensions? Using what criteria? After thinking about this awhile, Tiffany decides that because she does not have as many things as some of her rich friends she was a little cheated in her life. Why should they have more than she has?

Should Tiffany feel cheated? Is this a good way to judge fairness in life? What criterion should we use to decide this? Again, the answers are not so easy.

Each of these three friends, thus, used different definitions of "fair share" and came up with different answers to the question of the degree of fairness in their lives. Sam used a merit criterion, Juliet looked at need, and Tiffany endorsed an equality standard. All of these definitions can have validity in different situations and contexts, and deciding which one should take precedence may depend on the allocator's goals for distributing resources. Resources allocated on the basis of merit promote competition, hard work, and greater output; those given on the basis of need create feelings of care and compassion among recipients; and those distributed on the basis of equality build a sense of teamwork and solidarity among individuals. Can we reach all three of these goals simultaneously? This is usually difficult. And what happens if, as may have occurred with our three friends, there is a mismatch between our definitions of deservingness and the definitions that are used by those who have power over us? These were some of the issues we examined in Chapter 1 on distributive justice in this book.

Fair Process

Now let's shift our perspective a bit. Imagine that as two of your other friends, Tisha and Mathew, listen to the above discussion on deservingness, they assert that receiving lots of material things in their lives has never been important to them. Rather, they think of fairness more in terms of fair processes than fair outcomes. They are specifically concerned with some of the issues we raised in Chapter 2 on procedural justice. For example, despite the fact that she is quite wealthy, Tisha reflects that she never was really treated fairly in her life. She remembers that she was not taken seriously either personally or professionally and was never able to find her own true "voice." People, she believes, tended to ignore her and not listen to her ideas and opinions. Mathew, on the other hand, feels the opposite. Even though he never held a high-powered position or made a lot of money, he said he always felt appreciated and respected. This counted greatly to him, and he defines his life as being pretty fair, overall. Thus, he looks back on his life with few regrets whereas Tisha feels discontented and sad.

Tisha and Mathew, in our example, demonstrate how our perceptions that we experienced what we have called "fair process" in life can be just as important to us as our evaluations that we obtained our fair share of more tangible things. There may be many reasons why this is so, but one key factor seems to be that we want to be recognized as being important and as being a player in life, and not feel discounted and overlooked. This does not always mean that we are given lots of things, but rather that we are shown sufficient respect and regard. Being treated fairly in this sense means being treated like we matter, and that it turns out is hugely significant to many of us.

Retributive Justice

Now we will turn to another way of thinking about fairness. As our discussion with our friends continues let's imagine that two other of our companions, John and Peter, pipe up to offer their opinions. John and Peter have both have had multiple run-ins with the law. They have received numerous speeding and other traffic tickets over the course of their lives, and each had been arrested on a driving under the influence (DUI) charge. John was given a stiff fine for this and was made to take a 10-hour class on the dangers of drinking and driving. When Peter was arrested for DUI, on the other hand, he had his license taken away for a year, and he was made to serve a week in jail. This was the case even though it was his first DUI offense. Both John and Peter say that these experiences with the law are the main issue for them as they consider the fairness in their lives. Upon reflection John declares that, overall, he thinks he has been treated fairly in life. He comes to this conclusion because he feels that fair procedures were used to determine his guilt or innocence when he committed offenses, and that the punishment he received for them seemed appropriate to the nature of his actions. While not happy about the fines and penalties he had to pay, John thinks that he basically got what he deserved. Peter, on the other hand, states that he always felt targeted, discriminated against and subject to disproportionate and abusive treatment from those in power. He feels that his traffic arrests have often been quite arbitrary, and he considers that the time he had to spend in jail for his DUI offense was completely inappropriate. These perceptions have undermined Peter's respect for the law and his faith in our overall system of rules. All of this powerfully impacted his sense that he, unlike John, had been given a very raw and unfair deal in his life.

John and Peter, thus, looked at the idea of deservingness through a different type of lens than our previous friends. The kinds of definitions of deservingness they used were examined in Chapter 3 on retributive justice. Retributive justice is especially important as we think of fairness because it deals with our perceptions of those in power, and our trust in those who are designated by our society to keep order and to dispense justice impartially. If our trust in these authorities is eroded, the fabric of our society and the bonds that tie us together can become dangerously weakened and frayed. This, of course, diminishes our ability to create a well-functioning society. If we cannot trust those who have been appointed to protect us, whom can we trust?

Human Rights

Now let's imagine that the last person who remains in your group offers a fourth perspective on the meaning of justice to her. Your friend, Jen, says that when she considers this question of fairness she reflects on how she was impacted by government systems during her life. She ponders whether these systems provided her with sufficient services and support mechanisms to allow her to flourish. Just as importantly, she considers whether the government refrained from doing things that would hamper her, deny her freedom, and undermine her basic sense of worth. Jen concludes that she was treated fairly in all these regards. For instance, she remembers actively participating in political campaigns, freely expressing her opinions, protesting government actions that she did not agree with, practicing the religion of her choice, and being able to read and study whatever was of interest to her. She also remembers that she was not subjected to arbitrary arrest or to other forms of harassment from the state. She was, in short, treated in a manner that allowed her to pursue her passions in life and to maintain her dignity. This, she states, is enough for her.

We examined this question that Jen raised about the nature of the relationship between the individual and the larger state in Chapter 4 on societal justice. Societal Justice concerns the issue of how to structure a state in such a way as to support and enhance individuals' dignity and their sense of worth as human beings. In a just state, human striving should be facilitated so that individuals can pursue their potential unimpeded by others. To some people guaranteeing these types of protections may be the most important justice issue of all.

The Question of Fairness

So were your friends treated fairly in their lives? The answer, of course, rests on what they focus on. Their answers would additionally depend, in part, on how they define what counts as evidence for each of the questions they raise. Clearly, personal assessments of fairness will always be open to subjective interpretation, and will be dependent on where we choose to place our attention and how we decide to label our experiences. What is unacceptable to you may not be to me simply because as we think about it, we highlight different aspects of fairness. Thus, our conclusions about whether we received a fair deal in our lives will always remain to some degree in the eye of the beholder.

Can Society Ever Be Completely Fair?

We have seen how difficult it is to objectively answer questions such as "Has my life been fair?" Let's pose a slightly different inquiry now. That is, let's think about the degree to which complete societal justice is ever possible. What would such a society look like? How would we construct it?

We can consider this from a couple of perspectives. First, to build a perfectly just world we would have to agree about what standard we are going to use to measure fairness. As we saw from the above discussion, different questions yield different answers. For the purpose of this example, let's say that we decide to use a strict merit system to determine who receives what degree of rewards in life. Those who contribute more receive more, pure and simple. But could we ever structure an environment in which we could fairly implement this system? Could we agree on what constitutes a "contribution"? And even if we could agree on this, is it not the case that everyone would need to begin at the same starting point in life so that "merit" could be judged without giving some individuals unfair advantages? How would we do this? What if the house you were born in was bigger than mine and you had better teachers and mentors and access to more information than I did? If you ended up achieving more than me, would it be fair to say you earned your rewards more than I did?

Or we might imagine another society in which we want to treat everyone with great respect and in a manner that maintains their dignity.

Or maybe in a third society we agree to have a perfect criminal justice system put in place so when people violate the law they will receive a punishment that precisely matches the degree of harm they caused to others. Are such societies even possible? How would we implement our ideas of fairness? Who would get to decide, for instance, what was and what was not being treated with dignity? How would we enforce our fairness principles? These are not easy questions to answer.

Maybe We Do Not Need the Idea of Justice

We have talked about the importance of striving to create more fairness in life, and how hard it would be to create completely just societies. Let's look at this from a completely different angle. Perhaps somebody says to us that, of course, all this high-minded talk of fairness sounds quite inspirational, but is trying to create more fairness in life realistic or even laudable? Can we make too much of the whole idea of fairness? Some would we say we can. They might suggest, for instance, that by constantly framing things in fairness terms we undermine our ability to find satisfaction in life. Talking over and over about fairness may compel people to constantly compare their lot with others, and to filter their experiences through the lens of deservingness. We become experts at finding dimensions on which we have been treated unfairly. This may be a recipe for misery. Reflect on this a bit; think of a society in which fairness was not even a word or a concept. What would it be like? For instance, if we had efficient economic and social systems in place in which the large majority of the people were able to live comfortable lives, would this be enough?

If, as you reflected on a society without a concept of justice, you felt that something of great importance would be missing, you are not alone. Many people share this opinion. But why do we care so much about fairness. Why is it so important to us?

Fairness Is Important

If we think of what a good life might consist of we might think of a life in which we have a sufficient amount of material goods, efficient systems in which to conduct our business, kind leaders to guide us, daily pleasures to entertain us, and good friends and loving relationships to sustain us. Why is this not enough? Why do we have to make this murky by adding that we want things also to be fair?

We can answer this question in several ways. First, we may want our lives to be fair because we want a sense of deservingness in life. Beyond that, we want to feel that we matter in the eyes of others and that we are worthy of their respect. We want to think that we are not living in a random system and that if we do good things we will be rewarded and if we do bad things we will be punished (Lerner and Lerner 1981). In this way we may seek a kind of balance in our lives in which we hope to receive proportionate to what we give. Seeking fairness, thus, may be similar to seeking order and predictability in a potentially chaotic world. Seeking fairness may also inspire us to go beyond ourselves in our concerns and look to others with more compassion and care.

So is life fair? Not always. Can we structure completely fair societies? Probably not. But this does not mean the effort to try to do so is unimportant. Fairness goals, even if never completely achievable, can serve as aspirational guides that direct our behavior and motivate us to continually strive to improve our condition. It may be this process of striving itself, rather than the specific outcomes we achieve, which in the end is most important.

References

Lerner, Melvin and Sally Lerner, eds., 1981. *The Justice Motive in Social Behavior: Adapting to Times of Scarcity and Change*, New York, NY: Oxford University Press.

Sabbagh, Clara and Manfred Schmitt, eds. 2016. *The Handbook of Social Justice Theory and Research*, New York, NY: Springer.

About the Author

Virginia Murphy-Berman received her PhD in clinical psychology from Northwestern University, and she completed postdoctoral training in law and psychology at the University of Nebraska–Lincoln. She has published over 50 articles and books in the area of psychology. She has a special interest in the area of social justice and has published extensively on that topic, including articles on cross-cultural differences in perceptions of fairness, analyses of the fairness of different methods for allocating healthcare resources in society, and considerations of the therapeutic impact of justice processes. For the past 12 years, she has been a professor in the Psychology Department at Skidmore College in Saratoga Springs, New York. While at Skidmore, she regularly taught a seminar on the topic of psychological theories of social justice. She currently serves on the editorial board of the *American Journal of Orthopsychiatry*. She also has reviewed articles for the journals of *Social Justice Research*, the *Journal of Child Abuse and Neglect*, the *Journal of Applied Social Psychology*, *Basic and Applied Social Psychology*, *Journal of Psychology: Interdisciplinary and Applied*, the *International Journal of Psychology*, and many others. She has just recently retired.

Index

Accuracy, 41
American Declaration of
     Independence, 92
"An eye for an eye" justice, 65–66
Angriness, 2, 72
Atkins v. Virginia 2002, 73
Attributes, comparing, 2, 5

Bad luck, 19–20
Bias suppression, 40

Cairo Declaration of Human
     Rights, 94
Cognitive capacity of the
     offender, 73
Comparison process, 2–3
Comparison targets, choosing, 3
Constructionist approach to
     criminal justice, 63
Correctability, 41, 54
Cost–benefit analyses, 62

Death penalty, 59, 66, 73, 75, 81, 97
  in the United States, 76–79
Decision-making process, 35–37,
     40–41, 44, 48
Deprivation, sense of, 1
  comparison process, 2–3
  comparison targets, choosing, 3
  deservingness, sense of, 2, 3, 4
  egotistical deprivation, sense of, 4
  empowered, feeling, 3
  entitlement, 3
  fraternal deprivation, sense of, 4
  justification, sense of, 4
  negative emotions, 3
  "rising expectations", 4
  upset, feeling, 3
Deservingness
  sense of, 1, 2, 3–4, 5, 29, 90
  special cases of, 21

Dignity, 4, 15, 48, 54, 65, 89–90
  and fairness in common
     employee-employer work
     situation (case study), 46–47
  being treated with, 44–45
  process fairness and (case study), 47
Distributive fairness, sense of, 12, 24
Distributive justice, xix, 1, 35
  "the death tax" (application),
     26–27
  deprivation, sense of. *See*
     Deprivation, sense of
  deservingness, special cases of, 21
  distributive fairness, sense of, 24
  educational opportunities, access to
     (application), 28
  effort, 5–6
  equality, allocating on the basis of,
     7–8
  health care resources
     (application), 27
  luck. *See* Luck
  merit. *See* Merit
  need, allocating on the basis of, 8
  poor job performance, reactions
     for, 6–7
  privilege. *See* Privilege
  scope of justice concerns, 8–9
DNA evidence, 77

"Effective" punishment, 63
Effort, 5–6
  when we are young, 6
Egotistical deprivation, sense of, 4
Emotions, negative, 3
Empowered, feeling, 3
Entitlement, 2, 3, 18
Equality
  allocating on the basis of, 7–8
  case study, 11
Equally fair, being, 9

Equal opportunity, 21
  level playing field and, 14–15
Equity theory, 5
Ethicality, 41, 54
Executions, 77–78

Fairness, xviii
Fairness standards, 7, 13
  in a common type of legal violation
      (case study), 42–43
  equality, 7–8
  merit, 7
  need, allocating on the basis of, 8
  in a procedural process of
      determining ethics violations
      (case study), 43–44
  scope of justice concerns, 8–9
Fair play, 21
  and uneven outcomes, 15
Fair punishment, 75–76
Fair share, 1, 15, 18
Food versus freedom, 91–92
Fraternal deprivation, sense of, 4
French Enlightenment period, 88
Furman v. Georgia 1972, 76

Game, rules of, 40
  accuracy, 41
  bias suppression, 40
  correctability, 41
  ethicality, 41
  procedural consistency, 40
  representativeness, 41
Game analogy, 13–14
"Get tough on crime" philosophy, 62
Good luck, 18–19
Gregg v. Georgia 1976, 76
Guilty, feeling, 23, 69–71, 73

Halloween prank, 64
Human rights, nature of, 87, 89
  dignity, 89–90
  focusing on individual standing
      alone or individual embedded
      within the group, 94–96
  food versus freedom, thinking
      about, 91–92
  positive rights, 90–91

rights versus duties and religious
    obligations, 93–94
  and universal declaration, 88–89
Human Rights Commission, 89

Inequality, degree of, 16, 26
Intentionality of the offender at the
    time he/she committed the
    crime, 72–73
Interactional justice, 44
  dignity, being treated with, 44–45
  informational justice, 46

Jealousness, 2
"Just deserts"/"an eye for an eye"
    justice, 65–66
Justice
  concept of, xvii–xix
  types of, xix–xx
Justification, sense of, 4, 17–18

Legal guilt, 70–71, 75, 79
Legal insanity, 70–71
Level playing field, 14
  and equal opportunity, 14–15
Luck, 18
  bad luck, 19–20
  belief in, 20–21
  case study, 23–24
  equalitarian, 19
  good luck, 18–19

Make-up behaviors, 64
Merit, 5
  case study, 9–10
  evaluating, 6
  as a standard of distribution, 7
Misfortune, 19–20

Narcissistic personality traits, 18
Need
  allocating on the basis of, 8
  evaluation of (case study), 10–11
Negative emotions, 3

Offender
  cognitive capacity of, 73
  reforming/changing, 62–63

Opportunity privilege (case study), 22–23
Organizational justice, 37
Outcome inequalities, 15
Outcome-input ratio, 5
Outcome rights, 92
Overcompensation, sense of, 17

Participatory justice, 36
 voice, 36–37
 voice, trust building, and legitimacy, 39
 voice effects, 37–38
 voice effects, salience of, 38–39
Poor job performance, reactions for, 6–7
Positive rights, 90–91
Power, rights and, 98
Privilege, 11
 case study, 22–23
 defined, 12
 earning, 12–13
 "fair play" and uneven outcomes, 15
 level playing field and equal opportunity, 14–15
 opportunity privilege (case study), 22–23
 people's reactions to being privileged, 17–18
 privileged hiring (case study), 22
 resource distributions, outcomes of, 13–14
 and time, 16
Procedural consistency, 40
Procedural justice, xix, 35
 children testifying in court (application), 51–52
 dealing with suspected terrorists (application), 49–51
 dealing with victims of alleged rape (application), 53
 definition of, 35–36
 dignity and fairness in common employee-employer work situation (case study), 46–47
 fairness in a common type of legal violation (case study), 42–43

fairness in a procedural process of determining ethics violations (case study), 43–44
 interactional justice, 44–46
 participatory justice. See Participatory justice
 process fairness and dignity (case study), 47
 reason for caring about, 48–49
 rules of the game. See Game, rules of
Process fairness and dignity (case study), 47
Proportionality, sense of, 16
Punishment, appropriateness of, 67, 69
 cognitive capacity of the offender, 73
 guilty, feeling, 71
 intentionality of the offender at the time he/she committed the crime, 72–73
 legal guilt, 70–71
 sexual offense against a child (case study), 67–68
 student cheating (case study), 68–69
Punishment, purpose of, 61
 "effective" punishment, 63
 "an eye for an eye" justice, 65–66
 "get tough on crime" philosophy, 62
 reestablishing order in society, 66
 reforming or changing the offender, 62–63
 sending a symbolic message to society, 67
 to stop doing inappropriate/ unwanted behavior, 61–62
 victim's feelings, considerations of, 63–65

Reestablishing order in society, 66
Reform goal of punishment, 63
Religious obligations, rights versus duties and, 93–94
Representativeness, 41, 54

Resource distributions, outcomes of, 13–14
Restorative justice, 64–65, 75
Retributive justice, xix, 59
  death penalty in the United States, 76–79
  death to terrorists (application), 81–82
  definition of, 59–60
  fair punishment, 75–76
  intentionality in a criminal case (case study), 74–75
  issue of age in an incident (case study), 73–74
  punishment, appropriateness of. See Punishment, appropriateness of
  punishment, purpose of. See Punishment, purpose of
  sex offenders, case of (application), 82–83
  "victimless crimes" (application), 79–81
Rights and power, 87, 98
Rights documents, 87–91, 98–99
Rights of access, 91
Rights versus duties and religious obligations, 93–94
Rising expectations, 4
Roper v. Simmons 2005, 73

Scope of justice concerns, 8–9
Self-aggrandizement, 18
Self-fulfilling prophesy, 20
Sending a symbolic message to society, 67

Sense of justice/injustice, 1
Sexual offense against a child (case study), 67–68
Societal justice, xviii, xx, 87
  definition of, 87–88
  female circumcision, the case of (application), 100–101
  human rights, nature of. See Human rights, nature of
  human rights and integrated schooling (application), 102–103
  human rights and universal declaration, 88–89
  human rights in "prego" (application), 101–102
  rights and power, 98
  rights documents, 98–99
  universal rights, 96–97
Student cheating (case study), 68–69

Time, privilege and, 16

Unbiased, being, 9
Universal Declaration of Human Rights (UDHR), 88–89
Universal rights, 91, 96–97, 99, 104
Upset, feeling, 2–4, 63

Victim's feelings, considerations of, 63–65
Voice, 35–37
Voice, trust building, and legitimacy, 39
Voice effects, 37–38
  salience of, 38–39

OTHER TITLES FROM OUR PSYCHOLOGY COLLECTION

Children's Rights: Towards Social Justice
by Anne B. Smith

The Elements of Mental Tests, Second Edition
by John D. Mayer

College Student Psychological Adjustment:Exploring Relational Dynamics That Predict Success by Jonathan F. Mattanah

College Student Psychological Adjustment: Theory, Methods, and Statistical Trends by Jonathan F. Mattanah

Momentum Press is one of the leading book publishers in the field of engineering, mathematics, health, and applied sciences. Momentum Press offers over 30 collections, including Aerospace, Biomedical, Civil, Environmental, Nanomaterials, Geotechnical, and many others.

Momentum Press is actively seeking collection editors as well as authors. For more information about becoming an MP author or collection editor, please visit http://www.momentumpress.net/contact

Announcing Digital Content Crafted by Librarians

Momentum Press offers digital content as authoritative treatments of advanced engineering topics by leaders in their field. Hosted on ebrary, MP provides practitioners, researchers, faculty, and students in engineering, science, and industry with innovative electronic content in sensors and controls engineering, advanced energy engineering, manufacturing, and materials science.

Momentum Press offers library-friendly terms:

- perpetual access for a one-time fee
- no subscriptions or access fees required
- unlimited concurrent usage permitted
- downloadable PDFs provided
- free MARC records included
- free trials

The **Momentum Press** digital library is very affordable, with no obligation to buy in future years.

For more information, please visit **www.momentumpress.net/library** or to set up a trial in the US, please contact **mpsales@globalepress.com**.

www.ingramcontent.com/pod-product-compliance
Lightning Source LLC
Chambersburg PA
CBHW050532270326
41926CB00015B/3185